MORE
MAKING OUT IN
JAPANESE

T0125264

MORE
MAKING OUT IN
JAPANESE

Revised Edition Expanded

Todd Geers and Erika Hoburg
revised by **Elisha Geers**

TUTTLE Publishing
Tokyo | Rutland, Vermont | Singapore

The Tuttle Story: "Books to Span the East and West"

Our core mission at Tuttle Publishing is to create books which bring people together one page at a time. Tuttle was founded in 1832 in the small New England town of Rutland, Vermont (USA). Our fundamental values remain as strong today as they were then—to publish best-in-class books informing the English-speaking world about the countries and peoples of Asia. The world has become a smaller place today and Asia's economic, cultural and political influence has expanded, yet the need for meaningful dialogue and information about this diverse region has never been greater. Since 1948, Tuttle has been a leader in publishing books on the cultures, arts, cuisines, languages and literatures of Asia. Our authors and photographers have won numerous awards and Tuttle has published thousands of books on subjects ranging from martial arts to paper crafts. We welcome you to explore the wealth of information available on Asia at **www.tuttlepublishing.com**.

Published by Tuttle Publishing, an imprint of Periplus Editions (HK) Ltd.

www.tuttlepublishing.com

Copyright © 1988 Charles E. Tuttle Publishing Co. Inc.
Copyright © 2003, 2015 Periplus Editions (HK) Ltd.
Illustrations by Akiko Saito
All rights reserved.

ISBN 978-4-8053-1225-4
Distributed by:

Japan
Tuttle Publishing, Yaekari Building 3F
5-4-12 Osaki, Shinagawa-ku
Tokyo 141-0032, Japan
Tel: (81) 3 5437 0171
Fax: (81) 3 5437 0755
sales@tuttle.co.jp
www.tuttle.co.jp

North America, Latin America & Europe
Tuttle Publishing
364 Innovation Drive,
North Clarendon VT 05759-9436, USA
Tel: 1 (802) 773 8930
Fax: 1 (802) 773 6993
info@tuttlepublishing.com
www.tuttlepublishing.com

Asia Pacific
Berkeley Books Pte. Ltd.
61 Tai Seng Avenue #02-12
Singapore 534167
Tel: (65) 6280-1330
Fax: (65) 6280-6290
inquiries@periplus.com.sg
www.periplus.com

19 18 17 16   8 7 6 5 4 3   1605RR
Printed in China

TUTTLE PUBLISHING® is a registered trademark of Tuttle Publishing,
a division of Periplus Editions (HK) Ltd.

Contents

Introduction

So no one understands your Japanese? Worse yet, you don't understand theirs. You've planned your Saturday night, spent a week studying one phrase, and you can't wait to use it. You're at a club, armed with the latest edition of *Learn Japanese in 27-and-a-1/2-Minutes-a-Day* for moral support, and you lay the phrase on that good-looking local. What happens? The response isn't like in the book. Why?

Basically, because the Japanese don't play by the book when it comes to their daily language, just as Westerners don't. So what can you do? Well, you could give up and decimate your chances of getting with anybody, or you could learn to speak real Japanese.

Just as we speak in a relaxed, colloquial manner, so do the Japanese. On trains, in bars, during ball games, or when getting intimate with their partners, they all use shortcuts—it's only natural! If you want to talk the way the Japanese do, then you need to know what to say, how to say it, and when to say it.

And better still, you'll need to know the cultural context it all happens in. We've built in lots of little morsels to help you paint a picture of the real Japan as you go along—this book will be your roadmap on the path to love and satisfaction in Japan! Right then? Okay, let's go!

INFORMATION

It's tricky to teach the proper pronunciation of a foreign language in a book, so we're not going to try, hoping you've already got the basics. To help you out, though, we've joined two and sometimes three or four words together, to make compound words or phrases that are easier to pronounce. Most of them are hyphenated to highlight merged words, to emphasize the slang suffixes and particles, and to facilitate pronunciation and memorization.

For example, the components of **fuzakenaide-yo** (ふざけ ないでよ) are: **fuzake** (from **fuzakeru**), **naide** (command form of **arimasen**), and the (quite forceful) suffix -**yo**. We've written the compound phrase **fuzakenaide-yo** so that you won't pause while pronouncing it, but say it entirely in one breath; a pause would weaken the impact.

We're sure that you're familiar with the polite question forms **des-ka** ですか and **mas-ka** ますか. Forget them. Except for a few needed for talking to strangers, requesting services, etc., the rest have been dismissed. In informal speech, rising intonation takes the place of these forms. Thus, the final syllables of all words and phrases in this book ending with a question mark should be pronounced with the kind of rising intonation we give to the question "Right?"

Slang that is too faddish is not included in this book, because such words come and go too quickly. If you use old slang, the reaction of your Japanese date will likely be, "He thinks he's being cool speaking like that, but nobody says that anymore. Hah, hah!" So we've avoided hot slang—if it's out of date people will think that you're funny or square. But feel free to use what you pick up on the street.

VARIATIONS

The terms "boy" and "girl" are used throughout the book, and we're definitely referring to the post-puberty phase here. To eliminate the embarrassing problem of boys using girls' words or vice versa, we've indicated words suitable for use by girls and boys with the symbols ♀ and ♂ respectively. Other words and phrases not marked can be used by both sexes, and (b→g) means a boy should use it when talking to a girl. For example:

Don't be upset.	**Okoranaide.** ♀ 怒らないで。 **Okoruna-yo.** ♂ 怒るなよ。
Make me warm.	**Atatamete.** 暖めて。
You look beautiful.	**Kirei-dayo.** (b→g) きれいだよ。

But before you go thinking that boys' and girls' speech patterns are absolutely divided, stop a minute. Don't be shocked if you hear a girl using a quite masculine phrase (or vice versa). The gender gap in Japanese speech is narrowing, especially among young people, and there's nothing wrong with "borrowing" for impact or emphasis. In this book, we've made the distinction as a general guide to usage.

One thing you'll notice as you speak with the Japanese (especially if you move around) is that people's speech patterns vary wildly. We're not just talking about slang here, there are also big differences between regions and social groups. It's impossible for us to include all the variations (more on the regional ones later) of the phrases in this book, so we've gone a standard Japanese (**hyōjungo** 標準語) style, which everyone will understand and which you can adapt to the area you're living in.

Adaptation is really important—the phrases here might seem too harsh to some ears and too soft to others. Take your cues from the speech and reactions of people around you. If they warm to the way you're talking, great, otherwise think about the way they're taking it and adjust. If all else fails, ask—foreigners aren't expected to know everything!

JAPANESE-ENGLISH-JAPANESE-...

You'll have seen above that we've written Japanese phrases in two ways—in **rōmaji** (ローマ字—Western script, with lines above some vowels meaning long sounds) and in Japanese script with **furigana** (phonetic **hiragana** 平仮名 above the Chinese **kanji** 漢字) for an added challenge as you get better. But many phrases are written in another phonetic alphabet, **katakana** 片仮名. **Katakana** are mostly used for foreign words, and there are many of them in this book—for example, "batteries" are **batterī** バッテリー. Among other things, they're also used to write a few Japanese superlatives, such as **chō** 超 (amazing-ly/fantastic-ally).

When using **katakana**, life gets a bit tricky when you hit the limitations of the Japanese language. It has only one final consonant (**n**), so when the Japanese pronounce English words with other consonant endings, they have to tack on a vowel, usually a **u**. "Game" becomes **gēmu** ゲーム, "bed" becomes **beddo** ベッド, etc. With no final "r" sound, they usually use a long "a"; for example "locker" becomes **rokkā** ロッカー. And since there is no "l" at all, "r" is used instead.

There are a few introduced sounds that the Japanese can usually pronounce, and so they've created new ways of writing them. A "we" (as in "web") is written ウェ, and *v* sounds are written as ヴ followed by a **katakana** vowel, as in **va** ヴァ, **vi** ヴィ etc.—though the ability to pronounce the *v* varies greatly, especially between generations!

The Japanese enjoy using English words sporadically in their speech and you should do the same. With a little practice, it's easy to get the hang of how to "*katakana-ize*" an English word, that is, to pronounce it the way a Japanese would, strange as it might seem at first. As a foreigner, you'd be expected to use **katakana** words—so don't hold back!

As a reference point, the chart next page shows the basic **kana** in each alphabet.

There are a few more variations in readings to watch out for. Notables are the use of **ha** as the subject particle, in which case it's read **wa** (such as わたしは = **watashi-wa** = I am), and verbs ending in -**masu** ます, which we've romanized to -**mas**, because that's how you say it. You'll pick them all up as you go along.

THE BASIC HIRAGANA & KATAKANA CHARACTERS

a		i		u		e		o	
あ	ア	い	イ	う	ウ	え	エ	お	オ
ka		**ki**		**ku**		**ke**		**ko**	
か	カ	き	キ	く	ク	け	ケ	こ	コ
ga		**gi**		**gu**		**ge**		**go**	
が	ガ	ぎ	ギ	ぐ	グ	げ	ゲ	ご	ゴ
sa		**shi**		**su**		**se**		**so**	
さ	サ	し	シ	す	ス	せ	セ	そ	ソ
za		**ji**		**zu**		**ze**		**zo**	
ざ	ザ	じ	ジ	ず	ズ	ぜ	ゼ	ぞ	ゾ
ta		**chi**		**tsu**		**te**		**to**	
た	タ	ち	チ	つ	ツ	て	テ	と	ト
da		**ji**		**zu**		**de**		**do**	
だ	ダ	ぢ	ヂ	づ	ヅ	で	デ	ど	ド
na		**ni**		**nu**		**ne**		**no**	
な	ナ	に	ニ	ぬ	ヌ	ね	ネ	の	ノ
ha		**hi**		**fu**		**he**		**ho**	
は	ハ	ひ	ヒ	ふ	フ	へ	ヘ	ほ	ホ
ba		**bi**		**bu**		**be**		**bo**	
ば	バ	び	ビ	ぶ	ブ	べ	ベ	ぼ	ボ
pa		**pi**		**pu**		**pe**		**po**	
ぱ	パ	ぴ	ピ	ぷ	プ	ぺ	ペ	ぽ	ポ
ma		**mi**		**mu**		**me**		**mo**	
ま	マ	み	ミ	む	ム	め	メ	も	モ
ya				**yu**				**yo**	
や	ヤ			ゆ	ユ			よ	ヨ
ra		**ri**		**ru**		**re**		**ro**	
ら	ラ	り	リ	る	ル	れ	レ	ろ	ロ
wa								**o**	
わ	ワ							を	ヲ
n									
ん	ン								

 ▢ katakana characters

BEING CHOOSY

There are plenty of phrases for which the Japanese have alternatives, as in any language. As well as the boy/girl classification, we've listed them in a rough order from least to most casual, also getting rougher as they become more casual. If what you're saying doesn't seem to fit the mood, again, adapt to the speech of the people around you!

In the book, we've included the Japanese words for "me" and "you" in many phrases. In practice, they often leave them out, unless particular clarification is needed, but until you can instinctively understand who is being referred to, it's best to use them. If you do, there are a range of words available, not just the gender-neutral **watashi** 私 (with its super-formal counterpart **watakushi** 私) and **anata** あなた that textbooks love.

For girls, there's **atashi** あたし, and for guys there's **boku** 僕 and **ore** 俺. To say "you," girls can say **anata** あなた or **anta** あんた, and guys can say **kimi** 君 or **omae** 前. In this book, we've stuck with **anata** and **kimi**, because these are the "safest" for everyday conversation. **Omae** and **ore** in particular are very harsh, uncompromising words that can put people off. Until you know when best to use these words (again by the speech of the Japanese around you), steer clear!

STRESSED OUT OVER ENDINGS

One thing that we have to say is that in Japanese, how you say something can have more meaning than what you say. Think about it: when you're sharing an intimate moment, you can convey many emotions by sounding caring and serious, on top of what you're actually saying. Some phrases can be changed from statements to questions just by the tone or particle at the end... the list goes on. Here's a rundown of some slang endings and tonal tricks.

For starters, the rules say that plain negative verbs end in **-nai** (e.g. **wakaranai** 分からない I don't understand/know). But you'll hear other forms, like **-n**, as in **wakaran** 分からん, or **shiran** 知らん (I dunno) or special corruptions like **wakan'nai** 分かんない and **iu** 言う pronounced **yū** ゆう. (Plain positive forms generally don't change as they're pretty simple already.)

The most common slang final particle is **ne**, often lengthened to **nē**. Only partly fictitiously, it seems to us that when a newborn Japanese baby is shown off for the first time, someone will say **Kawaii-nē** かわいいね (Isn't he/she cute?), and inevitably the flock of admirers will all say **Nē!** ねえ! (Oh yes!). From such early exposure, the child is doomed to utter **nē** for the rest of his/her life.

Nē gives an (familiar yet) emphatic ending, usually a rhetorical question, and lengthening it adds more emphasis. With falling intonation it's more of an explanation. It isn't often said with a rising intonation, but can be said in a high pitch for emphasis. Girls prefer **ne** and **nē**, and guys have an alternative, **na**, which is used in the same way. But as we said before, the gap is narrowing, and, especially around women, guys will often use **ne**.

Other handy sentence endings (added to any form but the **mas** form) include **yo** よ, used to emphasise that "I'm telling you what I think (and you should do this)." **Wa** わ is often added by women to soften phrases, and you'll see it throughout this book. If you prefer a more blunt style, don't use it, or use **yo** instead. **-noda** 〜のだ (less formally **-nda** 〜んだ) makes the sentence a clear explanation, with a feeling, of "that's the way it is."

These can be combined liberally. For example, you're trying to decide which movie to see, and someone is being quite pushy about their choice. To be clear that you've already seen it and once was enough, you can say **Mō mitan--dayo-ne** もう見たんだよね。

Zo ぞ and **ze** ぜ can be added (usually by guys) to give instructions. **Zo** means "let's do..." as in **Yoshi, iku-zo** よし、行くぞ (Right, let's go), similar to but slightly harsher than **ikō** 行こう. **Ze** is a very strong command form, e.g. **Iku-ze!** 行くぜ！(Move it!) Finally, **-kke** is a handy ending, expressing either uncertainty or forgetfulness **Nan-datta-kke?** 何だったっけ？(What was it again...?)

The meaning of some phrases may be changed from a statement to a question by a rising final intonation, and these phrases are marked by diamonds (♦). For example:

Haven't seen you around for a while.	♦ **Hisashiburi-ne.** ♀ 久しぶりね。 ♦ **Hisashiburi-dane.** 久しぶりだね。

With a rising intonation, the sentence becomes "Haven't seen you around for a while, have I?"

And which parts of the phrase you stress also make a big difference—stressing a **yo** emphasizes that you're pushing your opinion. Stressing the **sō** in **sō-dane/sō des-ne** そうだ ね/そうですね (that's right) means you agree more strongly.

Finally, put emotion into your voice. You might think that the Japanese spoken around you is emotionless because it seems so fast, but nothing could be further from the truth. Put feeling into your voice as you would in English, and your message will be loud and clear.

THE LAST WORD

Does all of this sound really daunting? It shouldn't! Think of this introduction as a reference page for your journey through the Japanese-speaking world. Just keep these points in mind, and you'll find this book a valuable resource to speed your street Japanese skills along.

And there's one last thing: the Japanese love to see foreigners making an effort to speak Japanese! Through their troubles learning English, they know how hard it is, so even if you can't get the point across to start with, keep trying and you'll earn more respect. And if you're using real phrases like the ones in this book, all the better!

1

Getting to Know You

Hello! Hi!

Ohayō!
おはよう！
Kon'nichi-wa!
こんにちは！
Komban-wa!
こんばんは！

Ohayō! is used in the morning, say until 10 a.m., and with people you're seeing for the first time that day. **Kon'nichi-wa!** is for the daytime, and **Komban-wa!** for the evening. As everyday phrases, there are many variations and contractions of these, formal and informal, and they differ between regions of Japan—but these are the universal standards!

Hajimemashite
はじめまして。

This is a (somewhat formal) word you use to say hi to someone you haven't met before.

Allow us to introduce ourselves.	Atashitachi-no jikoshōkai sasete. ♀ あたしたちの自己紹介させて。 Bokutachi-no jikoshōkai sasete. ♂ 僕たちの自己紹介させて。
Would you introduce your friends?	Anata-no tomodachi-o shōkai shite? ♀ あなたの友達を紹介して？ Kimi-no tomodachi-o shōkai shite? ♂ 君の友達を紹介して？
I'm...	Atashi-wa... ♀ あたしは... Boku-wa... ♂ 僕は...

This is usually your first chance to practice katakana-ized pronunciation. It's sometimes a good idea to say your name in its original pronunciation first, and then in katakana form, which lets your new friend choose whether to try the "foreign version" or play safe with katakana—a choice they'll appreciate.

Where do you live?	Doko-ni sunderu-no? どこに住んでるの？
Where are you from?	Doko kara kitano? どこから来たの？
Where is your hometown?	Jimoto doko? 地元どこ？

| **Where do you come from?** | Dokkara kita-no?
どっから来たの？ |

Doko-ni sunderu-no? should be used if you are introduced by someone. If there is no introduction, both **Doko-ni sunderu-no?** and **Dokkara kita-no?** are okay and both produce the same answer. Girls might tell you their address, or they may just say **atchi** あっち , meaning "over there."

| **I'm from America/ the U.K./Australia/ New Zealand.** | Atashi-wa Amerika/Igirisu/ Ōsutoraria/Nyūjīrando-kara kita-no. ♀
あたしはアメリカ/イギリス/ オーストラリア/ニュージーランドから来たの。
Boku-wa Amerika/Igirisu/ Ōsutoraria/Nyūjīrando-kara kita. ♂
僕はアメリカ/イギリス/ オーストラリア/ニュージーランドから来た。 |

The Japanese don't have a word for Britain—**Igirisu** is it, and the distinction between England, Great Britain and the U.K. is usually lost on the Japanese. Those wanting to emphasise their Scottish or Welsh background can substitute **Sukottorando** スコットランド or **Uēruzu** ウェールズ .

| **How old are you?** | Nansai?
何歳？ |

To this question, girls will usually answer with **Atete!, Nansai-da-to omou?** あてて！何歳だと思う？ "Guess! How old do you think I am?," or **Ikutsu-ni mieru?** いくつにみえる？ "How old do I look?"

Are you an only child?	Anata hitorikko? ♀ あなた一人っ子?
	Kimi hitorikko? ♂ 君一人っ子?

Another way to ask this is:

Do you have any siblings?	Kyōdai-wa iruno? 兄弟はいるの?

Are you the oldest?	Anata ichiban ue? ♀ あなた一番上?
	Kimi ichiban ue? ♂ 君一番上?

Another way to ask this is:

Are you the oldest son/second son/youngest?	Chōnan/jinan/suekko? 長男／次男／末っ子?

Are you the oldest daughter/second daughter/youngest?	Chōjo/jijo/suekko? 長女／次女／末っ子?

Are you a student?	Gakusei? 学生?

The answer might be **kōkōsei** 高校生 (high school student) **daigakusei** 大学生 (university student), **sen-mon-gakkōsei** 専門学校生 (student of a specialist school–e.g. dental assistant, nurse...), **tandaisei** 短大生 (junior/two-year college student, almost all of whom are women).

What type of school?	Don'na gakkō? どんな学校?

I went to a regular/ special (trade) school.	**Atashi-wa-futsū-no/senmon gakkō-ni itta.** ♀ あたしは普通の／専門学校に行った。 **Boku-wa futsū-no/senmon gakkō-ni itta.** ♂ 僕は普通の／専門学校に行った。
Where are you studying? (i.e. at what institution)	**Doko-de benkyō shiteru-no?** どこで勉強してるの？
What do (did) you study at the university?	**Daigaku-de nani-o senkō shiteru (shita)-no?** 大学で何を専攻してる（した）の？

Senkō means "major study area."

Another way to ask this is:

What did you study in school?	**Daigaku-de nani benkyō shiteta-no?** 大学で何勉強してたの？
I did economics/law/ politics/English/ Spanish.	**Keizai/Hōritsu/Seiji/Eigo/ Supeingo-o benkyō shita.** 経済／法律／政治／英語／スペイン語を勉強した。
English Literature	**Eibungaku** 英文学

International Relations	Kokusai Kankeigaku 国際関係学
Business	Bijinesu ビジネス
Information Technology (IT)	Aitī アイティー
Marketing	Māketingu マーケティング
History	Rekishi 歴史

(The word for someone who studied a science-related subject is **rikei** (理系). The word for someone who studied an arts or humanities-related subject is **bunkei** (文系))

What club/sports team did you belong to/play on (in secondary school)?	Nani-bu datta-no? 何部だったの？
What club/sports team did you belong to/play on in college?	Sākuru wa nani shiteta-no? サークルは何してたの？

Sākuru サークル : Kind of like a club in college. Your social life is largely determined by which "circle" you decide to join. If it's a hobby, chances are, a "circle" exists for it, especially at bigger universities. These "circles" can be centered around anything from Anime to football to gardening. In April when school starts, upperclassmen aggressively recruit freshmen to join their circle. Like fraternities/sororities, there is some light hazing and usually some amount of drinking involved. You can use it to pursue a passion, make friends, or meet girls/guys.

What's your job?	Shigoto nani shiten-no? 仕事何してんの？
How do you spend your time?	Itsumo nani shiten-no? いつも何してんの？
Will you be my Japanese teacher?	Atashi-ni nihongo oshiete-kureru? ♀ あたしに日本語教えてくれる？ Boku-ni nihongo oshiete-kureru? ♂ 僕に日本語教えてくれる？
I'll teach you English.	Atashi-ga eigo oshiete ageru. ♀ あたしが英語教えてあげる。 Boku-ga eigo oshiete ageru. ♂ 僕が英語教えてあげる。

Pithy as these sound to Western ears, the Japanese often say things like this and like to hear them—even if they're only a prelude to more conversation!

Have I seen you before?	Mae-ni (atta-koto) atta-kke? 前に（会ったこと）あったっけ？ Mae-ni atta-koto nai? 前に会ったことない？

You come here often, don't you?	Koko-ni yoku kuru-yone? ここによく来るよね？
I've been watching you.	Anata-no-koto zutto mitetano-yo. ♀ あなたのことずっと見てたのよ。 Kimi-no-koto zutto mitetanda-yo. ♂ 君のことずっと見てたんだよ。

It's better to soften these two phrases into "semi-questions" by using a rising intonation.

You're really pretty.	Kimi-tte hontō-ni kawaii-ne. ♂ 君って本当にかわいいね。
You're handsome.	Anata-tte sugoku kakkoii. ♀ あなたってすごくかっこいい。 Suteki-dane. ♂ すてきだね。
You're fascinating.	Anata-tte miryokuteki. ♀ あなたっては魅力的。 Kimi-tte miryokuteki-dane. ♂ 君って魅力的だね。
I want to know more about you.	Anata-to motto hanashitai. ♀ あなたともっと話したい。 Kimi-to motto hanashitai. ♂ 君ともっと話したい。

Though this literally means "I want to talk with you more," it's softer than the phrases below, and so is more suited to someone you've only met recently.

Anata-no-koto motto shiritai. ♀
あなたのこともっと知りたい。

Kimi-no-koto motto shiritai. ♂
君のこともっと知りたい。

Come on, tell me more.	**Ii-janai. Motto oshiete-yo.** いいじゃない。もっと教えてよ。
You don't talk very much.	**Anata-wa anmari shaberanai-none.** ♀ あなたはあんまりしゃべらないのね。 **Kimi-wa anmari shaberanai-ne.** ♂ 君はあんまりしゃべらないね。
Nice/That's cool/ I like that.	**Ii-nē.** 良いねえ。
Man, you really are aggressive!	**Gan-gan osu-ne!** がんがん押すね!
Are you shy?	**Hitomishiri-nano?** 人見知りなの?
Don't be shy.	**Hazukashi-garanai-de.** 恥ずかしがらないで。

Also means "Don't be embarrassed."

Ask me some questions.	Nanka kiite. 何か聞いて。
Ask me anything you want.	Nandemo kiite-ii-yo. 何でも聞いていいよ。
Except what color underwear I'm wearing.	Nani iro-no shitagi-o tsuketeruka-wa oshienai kedo. 何色の下着をつけてるかは教えないけど。
I like your personality.	Anata-no seikaku suki-yo. ♀ あなたの性格好きよ。 Kimi-no seikaku suki-dayo. 君の性格好きだよ。
You're my type.	Anata atashi-no (suki-na) taipu. ♀ あなたあたしの(好きな)タイプ。 Kimi boku-no (suki-na) taipu. ♂ 君僕の(好きな)タイプ。 Kimi-wa boku-no konomi. ♂ 君は僕の好み。
What kind of people do you like?	Don'na hito-ga suki? どんな人が好き？ Don'na hito-ga taipu? どんな人がタイプ？

| **I kinda like people like (you/that).** | **Sōiu seikaku sukikamo.** ♂
そういう性格好きかも。 |

You can substitute the subsequent words into the following sentence:

| **I like...type of person.** | **...hito-ga ii.**
…人がいい。 |

quiet:	**otonashii** おとなしい
	mukuchi-na 無口な
loud:	**nigiyaka-na** にぎやかな
tender:	**yasashii** 優しい
funny:	**omoshiroi** 面白い
tough:	**tafu-na** タフな
serious/dedicated:	**majime-na** 真面目な
considerate:	**omoiyari-no aru** 思いやりのある
cheerful:	**genki-na (-no aru)** 元気な (のある)
rich:	**okane-mochi-no** お金持ちの
shy:	**hazukashigari-ya-na** 恥ずかしがりやな
bright:	**akarui** 明るい

elite:	**erīto-na** エリートな
manly:	**otokoppoi/otokorashii** 男っぽい／男らしい
feminine:	**on'nappoi/on'narashii** 女っぽい／女らしい
outgoing:	**shakōteki-na** 社交的な
smart:	**atama-no ii** 頭のいい
glamorous:	**guramā-na** グラマーな
chubby:	**potchari-shita** ぽっちゃりした
slim:	**yaseteru** やせてる
thin-waisted:	**uesto-ga hosoi** ウエストが細い
big:	**ōkii** 大きい
big eyes:	**me-ga ōkii** 目が大きい
small:	**chiisai** 小さい
small butt:	**oshiri-no chiisai** お尻の小さい
small breasts:	**mune-no chiisai** 胸の小さい
small mouth:	**kuchi-no chiisai** 口の小さい
long hair:	**kami-no nagai** 髪の長い
long legs:	**ashi-no nagai** 足の長い

pretty teeth:	ha-no kirei-na 歯のきれいな
cute:	kawaii かわいい
cute smile:	egao-no kawaii 笑顔のかわいい
sexy:	sekushī-na セクシーな
sporty:	supōtī-na スポーティーな
I like girls who are strong.	Tsuyoki-na on'na-no-ko suki-dayo. 強気な女の子好きだよ。
I kinda like guys who are a little aggressive.	Oshi-ga tsuyoi hito kirai janai-yo. 押しが強い人嫌いじゃないよ。

Ikemen イケメン: good-looking guy.

Bijin 美人: good looking girl.

Oshare-na hito/ko オシャレな人／子: someone fashionable (**ko**: usually to refer to girls; **hito**: usually to refer to guys)

Nori-no-ii hito/ko ノリのいい人／子: someone who can keep up, is outgoing and fun in a social situation.

Moriagete-kureru hito/ko 盛り上げてくれる人／子: someone who makes a party lively or exciting.

Kikubari jōzu-na hito/ko 気配り上手な人／子: someone

who is considerate, someone who makes sure everyone is comfortable and having a good time in a social situation.

Matcho-na hito マッチョな人: someone who is muscular, built, stacked.

Taiikukai-kei-no hito/ko 体育会系の人／子 someone who used to play sports in school, has a sporty look and attitude.

Kashikoi hito/ko 賢い人／子: someone who is smart.

Interi-na kanji-no hito/ko インテリな感じの人／子: someone who gives off an air of intelligence.

Hōyōryoku-no aru hito 包容力のある人: someone who is financially set. A word that comes up in conversation among girls when describing men they want to marry.

Ryōri-ga dekiru hito/ko 料理が出来る人／子: someone who is good at cooking.

Mendōmi-ga-ii hito/ko 面倒見がいい人／子: someone who nurturing or taking care of others.

Shikkari shiteru hito/ko しっかりしてる人／子: someone who is independent, strong.

Sutairu-ga-ii hito/ko スタイルがいい人／子: someone who has a nice body, is fit.

When young men are talking about girls their age they usually say 子 **ko** (child) instead of 人 **hito** (person). When young girls are talking about guys their age, they use 人 **hito**. If they are talking about a younger member of the opposite sex, kind of in a big sisterly kind of way, she might use 子 **ko**. However, once in their 30's, both men and women refer to members of the opposite sex with 人. Women often refer to their husbands as うちの人 **uchi no hito**, literally "the person in my home."

Other third person pronouns:

Aitsu あいつ: that guy/girl.

Yatsu ヤツ: that guy/girl (kind of in jest or being funny).

Yarō 野郎: that guy (can be more like "jerk" or "asshole" depending on the tone and context).

Don't look so suspicious!	Son'na-ni keikai shinaide-yo. そんなに警戒しないでよ。
That's hilarious!	Ukeru! ウケる！
Are you serious/ for real?	Maji-de? マジで？
I like your hairstyle.	Anata-no heasutairu ga suki. ♀ あなたのヘアスタイルが好き。 Kimi-no heasutairu ga suki. 君のヘアスタイルが好き。
Do you follow the latest fads?	Hayari-ni noru? はやりに乗る？
What's popular now?	Ima nani-ga hayatteru-no? 今何がはやってるの？

You have good taste in clothes.	Fuku-no sensu-ga ii-ne. 服のセンスがいいね。 Fuku no sensu-ga ii-na. ♂ 服のセンスがいいな。
I'm not very stylish.	Atashi-wa anmari sutairisshu/oshare-janai. ♀ あたしはあんまりスタイリッシュ／おしゃれじゃない。 Boku-wa ammari ssutairisshu/oshare-janai. ♂ 僕はあんまりスタイリッシュ／おしゃれじゃない。

Said especially of clothes.

Will you give me some advice?	Nani-ka adobaisu shite-kureru? 何かアドバイスしてくれる？
Shall we go shopping together someday?	Kondo issho-ni shoppingu/kaimono-ni ikanai? 今度一緒にショッピング／買い物に行かない？
I don't like to shop alone.	Hitori-de shoppingu/kaimono suru-no-wa suki-janai. 一人でショッピング／買い物するのは好きじゃない。
Do you have a steady boy/girlfriend?	Tsukiatteru-hito iru? 付き合ってる人いる？

You must be very popular.	Moteru-deshō. ♀ もてるでしょう。 Moteru-darō. ♂ もてるだろう。
You must have many girlfriends/boyfriends. (You must be popular.)	Kanojo ippai irun-deshō. ♀ 彼女いっぱいいるんでしょう。 Kareshi ippai irun-darō. ♂ 彼氏いっぱいいるんだろう。
You must have a girlfriend.	Kanojo irun-deshō. ♀ 彼女いるんでしょう。
You must have a boyfriend.	Kareshi irun-darō. ♂ 彼氏いるんだろう。

The nuance is "You're good-looking, so I think you must have a steady girlfriend/boyfriend." Use these phrases to check if they are available without coming right out and asking!

Yes, I had one, but we broke up recently.	Un, demo, saikin wakareta. うん、でも、最近別かれた。
I've never been out on a date with a Japanese person.	Nihonjin-to dēto shita-koto ga nai. 日本人とデートしたことがない。
I've never been in a relationship with a Japanese person.	Nihonjin-to tsukiatta-koto-ga nai. 日本人と付き合った事がない。

Will you go out with me?	**Atashi-to dekakenai?** ♀ あたしと出かけない？ **Boku-to dekakenai?** ♂ 僕と出かけない？
Do you believe in destiny?	**Unmeitte shinjiru?** 運命って信じる？
If I hadn't taken that train/gone to that bar, we wouldn't have met.	**Ano densha-ni nora-nakatta-ra/ano bā-ni ika-nakatta-ra atashi-tachi awa-nakattan-dane.** ♀ あの電車に乗らなかったら／あのバーに行かなかったらあたしたち会わなかったんだね。 **Ano densha-ni nora-nakatta-ra/ano bā-ni ika-nakatta-ra boku-tachi awa-nakattan-dane.** ♂ あの電車に乗らなかったら／あのバーに行かなかったら僕たち会わなかったんだね。
Let's do this again.	**Mata kore shiyō.** またこれしよう。
Let's get together later.	**Ato-de mata-ne.** 後でまたね。

This means "Let's separate now and get back together later (today)."

Let's see each other again.	Mata aō-ne. また会おうね。
Let's meet on Tuesday at your favorite café.	Kayōbi-ni anata-no okiniiri-no kafe-de aō. ♀ 火曜日にあなたのお気に入りのカフェで会おう。 Kayōbi-ni kimi-no okiniiri-no kafe-de aō. ♂ 火曜日に君のお気に入りのカフェで会おう。
I'm glad we met.	Aete yokatta. 会えてよかった。
It'd be great to see you again.	Mata aeruto ureshii-na. また会えると嬉しいな。

If a girl adds, **na** 〜な , it usually sounds like of cuter. Guys can also use this too, but it doesn't make them sound feminine especially. It depends on the intonation, tone of voice, and body language. Using **na** 〜な has an element of the person hoping that event, in this case another date, will happen.

What shall we do now?
Ima-kara dō-suru?

What do you like to do?
Itsumo nani shiteru-no?

Shall we go shopping?
Shoppingu-ni ikō-ka?

We have plenty of time.
Jikan-ga ippai aru.

I like going to cafes.
Kafe-ni iku-no-ga suki.

COFFEE

Roppongi

Ginza

Harajuku

Let's go shopping!
Kaimono shiyō!

Fashion♪

Let's get out of here.
Deyō-yo.

2

Fun and Games

Are you busy right now?	Ima isogashii? 今忙しい?
What shall we do now?	Ima-kara dō suru? 今からどうする?
What do you like to do?	Itsumo nani shiteru-no? いつも何してるの?
I like...	...-ga suki. ...が好き。
going to karaoke	karaoke-ga suki カラオケが好き
going to clubs	kurabu-ni iku-no-ga suki クラブに行くのが好き
going to cafes/ coffee shops	kafe-ni iku-no-ga suki カフェに行くのが好き
going for walks	osampo suru-no-ga suki お散歩するのが好き

taking pictures	shashin toru-no-ga suki 写真取るのが好き
playing soccer	sakkā yaru-no-ga suki サッカーやるのが好き
going shopping	kaimono suru-no-ga suki 買い物するのが好き
going to the beach	umi-ni iku-no-ga suki 海に行くのが好き
going to art museums	bijutsukan-ni iku-no-ga suki 美術館に行くのが好き
going to drinking parties	nomikai-ni iku-no-ga suki 飲み会に行くのが好き
I want to go to...	...-ni ikitai. ...に行きたい。
What do you want to do?	Anata-wa nani-ga shitai-no? ♀ あなたは何がしたいの？ Kimi-wa nani-ga shitai? ♂ 君は何がしたい？
What do your friends want to do?	Anata-no tomodachi-wa nani-ga shitai-no? ♀ あなたの友達は何がしたいの？ Kimi-no tomodachi-wa nani-ga shitai? ♂ 君の友達は何がしたい？
Let's (all) go out together.	Min'na-de dekake-yō. 皆で出かけよう。
Let's get out of here.	Deyō-yo. 出ようよ。

As in "let's leave this building," when making plans to go out. Naturally, the assurance of going in a group is one way to get a reluctant potential date to agree!

It'll be a lot of fun.	Zettai tanoshii-yo. 絶対楽しいよ。
Let's go to the beach.	Umi-ni ikō. 海に行こう。
Let's go to a baseball/ soccer game.	Yakyū/Sakkā-no shiai-ni ikō. 野球／サッカーの試合に行こう。

Baseball is the most popular spectator sport in Japan, with several teams commanding strong support—the Yomiuri Giants in particular have a massive fan base spread throughout Japan. But baseball's support base is aging, and more and more young Japanese are into J.League (pro) soccer and Major League baseball.

What's the local team (here)?	(Kono hen-no) hōmutaun chīmu-wa nani/doko? (この辺の)ホームタウンチームは何／どこ？
I play/played baseball/ soccer back home.	Mukō-de yakyū/sakkā-o yaru/yatteta-yo. 向こうで野球／サッカーをやる／やってたよ。

Is it true that soccer is now more popular than baseball in Japan?	Saikin Nihon-dewa yakyū yori sakkā-ga ninkitte hontō? 最近日本では野球よりサッカーが人気って本当？
Let's cheer on the local team.	Jimoto-no chēmu-o ōen shiyō. 地元のチームを応援しよう。
I've always wanted to go to Koshien Stadium/ the Tokyo Dome...	Itsumo Kōshien Kyūjō/ Tōkyō Dōmu-ni itte mitai-na! いつも甲子園球場／東京ドームに行ってみたいな！

Koshien (in Kobe) is famous throughout Japan (and East Asian baseballing circles) as the home of Japanese baseball.

actor	haiyū 俳優
actor/performer	yakusha 役者
actress	joyū 女優
TV personality	tarento タレント
singer	kashu 歌手
music group	gurūpu グループ
band	bando バンド

Go! Go for it! (Good luck!)	Gambatte! 頑張って！
	Gambare! 頑張れ！

Gambare! is stronger, and is used in any situation (speaking directly to someone who is about to sit a test/play sport, cheering for your favorite team, encouraging runners in a marathon...). **Gambatte** is usually only used when speaking directly to someone.

Who is that (player)?	**Are/Ano senshu dare?** あれ／あの選手だれ？
Let's watch a movie.	**Eiga-o miyō-yo.** 映画を見ようよ。
Who is your favorite actor/actress?	**Yūmeijin-de dare-ga suki?** 有名人で誰が好き？

Yūmeijin means "a famous person," so this is a broadly useful phrase.

Did you see...?	**...mita?** ...見た？
I saw (it).	**Mita-mita!** 見た見た！

In Japanese, you can say a phrase like 見た twice for emphasis. It's used by both genders. Depending on the tone, though, it can mean excitement, as in this case, or annoyance (imagine in English: alright *alright!*)

	Mita. 見た。
	Mita-yo. 見たよ。
I haven't seen it (yet).	**Mada mitenai.** (まだ)観てない。
look	**miru** 見る

watch (a movie)　　　miru
　　　　　　　　　　　　観る

I couldn't see (it).　　Mie-nakatta.
　　　　　　　　　　　　見えなかった。

When you can't see something because something else is in the way, or because you didn't have the chance to go to the movies.

　　　　　　　　　　　　Mi(ra)re-nakatta.
　　　　　　　　　　　　見(ら)れなかった。

When you can't see something because of your own lack of vision or perception.

Do you want to see...?　Mitai?
　　　　　　　　　　　　見たい?

Shall we go and　　　Mite miyō-ka?
watch it?　　　　　　見てみようか?

This is of course a good phrase when thinking about movies.

What time does the　　Tsugi-no-wa nanji (des-ka)?
next [movie, game　　次のは何時(ですか)?
etc.] start?

It's better to add **des-ka** when talking to the likes of shop-keepers and ticket sellers—using casual language may make them less helpful.

We have plenty of time. Jikan nara tappuri aru.
　　　　　　　　　　　　時間ならたっぷりある。

　　　　　　　　　　　　Jikan-ga ippai aru.
　　　　　　　　　　　　時間がいっぱいある。

The movies in Japan are quite expensive, and with most theaters downtown, are not such a popular option for people in the suburbs. With the proliferation of home theater systems, many people now rent movies instead.

Shall we get a video/ DVD (instead)?	(Sono kawari) Bideo/ DVD-o karite miyō-ka? (その代わり)ビデオ／DVDを 借りて見ようか？
Do you know a good place (near here)?	Konohen-no iitoko shitteru? この辺の良いとこ知ってる？
I know (a good place).	(Ii tokoro) wakaru(-yo). (良い所)分かる(よ)。

There are of course plenty of other socializing opportunities, with perhaps the most common being karaoke, shopping and relaxing at parks. Of course, there's also the option of clubbing, eating and drinking.

A casual evening or night out in Japan will often involve karaoke. Karaoke literally means "without orchestra," and this popular activity usually takes place in special karaoke bars, found throughout cities especially at major railway stations and entertainment areas. The "bars" are collections of many rooms, where you can sing, eat and drink in relative privacy. (The Japanese take their leisure very seriously!)

Karaoke is an activity enjoyed by people of all ages in Japan. Unlike karaoke in the United States, which usually takes place in bars or other adult establishments, "karaoke boxes" in Japan is open to anyone. Rates depend on the time of day and day of the week, the most expensive time being Friday or Saturday evenings. Usually you have the choice of adding a "all-you-can-drink" option, soft drinks for minors, alcoholic beverages included for people over 20. Many of the chain karaoke boxes have a good selection of foreign music as well as Japanese music. If you are in Japan for a longer stay, it may be a good idea to sign up for a member's card, which gets you a lower rate.

Some karaoke etiquette:

1) Take turns singing. Don't hog the mic!

2) Make sure everyone has a full drink. Karaoke rooms usually have a phone with which you can place orders. If you are doing an all-you-can-drink, you want to get your money's worth! Usually one person is the designated drink-orderer.

3) When they are ordering, of course you can request a drink, but it's also nice to see if your neighbor would like a refill.

4) Listen to other people singing. Even if you're with a group of friends, it's still important to be supportive of your fellow karaoke-ers. Clap or sing along, or bust out the tambourine!

5) Try to read the "atmosphere" when choosing music. Are you in the company of fellow foreigners who like rock music? A bunch of Japanese metal heads? Unless you know everyone has similar tastes in music as you, mainstream or American pop music is always a safe bet. Or you can try and sing a Japanese song, which never seizes to impress the Japanese.

6) Pay up. Unless you are in a group of only foreigners, Japanese people usually go Dutch, regardless of what

you ate/drank. This is why all-you-can drink or course meals are popular. It is easier to calculate, and everyone pays the same amount.

Do you like karaoke?	Karaoke suki? カラオケ好き？
Let's sing karaoke.	Karaoke utaō/ikō. カラオケ歌おう／行こう。
What shall we sing first?	Mazu-wa nani-ni shiyō-ka? まずは何にしようか？
You choose the first song (You go first).	(Saki-ni) dōzo. (先に)どうぞ。

This phrase can be used in a variety of situations, from allowing someone to pass through first to letting them pay before you at the cashier. It is of course a sign of good manners and a good way to kick off any communal activity.

Are there any English songs?	Eigo-no-uta aru? 英語の歌ある？
I don't know how to work the machine.	Irekata wakaranai. 入れ方分からない。
That person's/John's singing is funny/ interesting.	Ano-ko/hito/Jon-no utaikata omoshiroi. あの子／人／ジョンの歌い方面白い。
Shall we sing something together?	Issho-ni utaō-ka? 一緒に歌おうか？

Your singing is really good.	(Uta) jōzu-dane. (歌)上手だね。 (Uta) umai-ne. (歌)うまいね。

It's important to compliment the efforts of others, expecially when they are really good, but you'll also likely be complimented yourself—especially if you try singing in Japanese! A hurried and embarrassed denial (**iie, iie** いいえ、いいえ) or thank you (**Aa, dōmo** ああ、どうも) are good ways to reply.

Shall we go shopping?	Shoppingu/kaimono-ni ikō-ka? ショッピング／買い物に行こうか？
I want to look around.	Mite mawaritai. 見て回りたい。
Let's go shopping in Roppongi/Ginza/ Harajuku/Shibuya	Roppongi/Ginza/Harajuku/ Shibuya de kaimono shiyō. 六本木／銀座／原宿／渋谷で買い物しよう。

Roppongi and Ginza have more expensive, high-end stores, while Shibuya and Harajuku are for younger, hipper shoppers. The Yoyogi Flea Market and other local flea markets are also good shopping options for the financially limited or adventurous.

I want to go shopping for clothes.	Yōfuku-o kaitai. 洋服を買いたい。
Let's go to Yamashita Park.	Yamashita Kōen-e ikō. 山下公園へ行こう。

I hear it's a good
spot for a date.

Dēto-spotto-datte kiita.
デートスポットだって聞いた。

Let's go to the
park again.

Mata kōen-ni ikō.
また公園に行こう。

I love to hold your
hand as we walk
through the park.

Anata-to te-o tsunaide
kōen-o aruku-no-ga suki. ♀
あなたと手をつないで公園を
歩くのが好き。

Kimi-to te-o tsunaide kōen-
o-aruku-no-ga suki. ♂
君と手をつないで公園を歩く
のが好き。

I came here by car.

Kuruma-de kita.
車で来た。

Would you like to go
for a drive?

Doraibu-ni ikitai?
ドライブに行きたい？

Don't worry, I'm a
good driver.

Unten umai kara daijōbu-
dayo.
運転旨いから大丈夫だよ。

I have room for two
more of your friends.

Anata-no tomodachi
futari-bun-no heya-mo
aru-yo. ♀
あなたの友達二人分の部屋
もあるよ。

Kimi-no tomodachi futari-
bun-no heya-mo aru-yo. ♂
君の友達二人分の部屋もある
よ。

3

Eating and Drinking

Would you like something to eat/drink?	Nani-ka taberu/nomu? 何か食べる？／飲む？
Let's get some food.	Nani-ka tabeyō. 何か食べよう。

A general invitation to get some food, at a buffet or à la carte.

	Tabemono tanomō. 食べ物頼もう。

When inviting someone to order food.

The menu, please.	Menyū-o kudasai. メニューをください。
What do you want?	Nani-ga ii? 何がいい？

Have you decided?	**Kimeta?** 決めた？
I can't decide what to eat.	**Nani tabete ii-ka wakaranai.** 何食べていいか分らない。
I'll order (for us).	**Atashi-ga ōdā suru/ shite-ageru.** ♀ あたしがオーダーする／してあげる。 **Boku-ga ōdā suru/ shite-ageru.** ♂ 僕がオーダーする／してあげる。
I'll buy it.	**Atashi-ga kau-yo.** ♀ あたしが買うよ。 **Boku-ga kau-yo.** ♂ 僕が買うよ。

This has the connotation of "I'll hand over the money, but we're (probably) paying our own shares."

> **Gochisō-suru.** ♀ / ♂
> ごちそうする。
> **Ogoru-wa.** ♀
> おごるわ。
> **Ogoru-yo.** ♂
> おごるよ。

This means "I'm paying for yours"—literally "let me treat you."

Food, especially at **izakayas**, or Japanese style pubs, are often shared amongst friends. If you are with people you just met, it's a good idea to use serving chopsticks if they're available. If you're with friends, you can ask if it's okay if you use your chopsticks. You can say:

Is it okay if I use my chopsticks?	Jikabashi-demo ii des-ka? 直箸でも良いですか？
Should we ask for some serving chopsticks?	Toribashi tanomi-mas-ka? 取り箸頼みますか？
I/You forgot the chopsticks/forks/knives/spoons.	Ohashi/fōku/naifu/supūn wasureta. お箸／フォーク／ナイフ／スプーン忘れた。

There are many rules governing the use of chopsticks. You shouldn't pass food from one set of chopsticks to another, because the Japanese place the ashes of their deceased into a funeral urn this way. It's also extremely offensive to stand chopsticks in a bowl of rice, as this is how food is offered to the spirits of the deceased. Plus, chopsticks should never be grasped in the fist as this is how they would be held for use as a weapon, and it is poor manners to lick them.

That said, once mastered, using chopsticks is second nature, and correct technique and etiquette can get you considerable admiration. If you don't know how, get your Japanese friends to teach you!

Try this!	(Kore) tabete-mite. (これ)食べてみて。
What's it called?	Nante iu-no? 何て言うの？

I've never tried...	...tabeta kotonai. …食べたことない。
What's you favorite Japanese food?	Nihon-no tabemono-de, nani-ga ichiban suki? 日本の食べ物で、何が一番好き？
Can you eat nattō/ anko?	Nattō/anko taberareru? 納豆／あんこ食べられる？

Nattō is fermented soybeans, which are stringy and foul-smelling. Anko is the general name for sweet soybean paste, and like nattō is often unpalatable to foreigners.

Yes, I can.	Un, tabe(ra)reru(-yo). うん、食べ(ら)れる(よ)。

This is less grammatical but more familiar (and shorter!) expression.

No, I can't.	Uun, tabe(ra)renai. ううん、食べ(ら)れない。
(That) looks delicious.	(Are) oishisō. (あれ)おいしそう。
It smells good.	Ii nioi. いいにおい。
Give me a bit more.	Mōchotto/Mōsukoshi chōdai. もうちょっと／もう少しちょうだい。

I'm still hungry.	Mada onaka suiteru. まだお腹空いてる。
Enough.	Jūbun./Tariru. 充分。／足りる。
Enough?	Tarita? 足りた?
Not enough.	Tarinai. 足りない。
(Sorry,) I can't eat that.	(Sumimasen,) Sore tabe(ra)renai. (すみません)それ食べ(ら)れ ない。
Itadakimas!	Itadakimas! いただきます!

Almost every Japanese says this before eating. The closest English equivalent is "grace," but without its religious meaning (of receiving from the gods). Don't hesitate to say this, and you may even be complimented on your good manners!

What do you think (about this)?	(Kore-ni tsuite) dō-mou? (これについて)どう思う?
Does this taste good?	Kore oishii? これおいしい?
It tastes good.	Oishii(!) おいしい(!)

Oishii is a grossly overused word, which can be voiced with the full gamut of emotions, from enthusiasm to indifference (meaning that it may not be good at all!). The Japanese indicate how they feel by the emotion they put into **oishii**. You can add other words, such as **kekkō oishii** 結構おいしい ("it's really good," even without much enthusiasm), but just saying **oishii** and meaning it is usually enough.

It's an unusual taste.	**Fushigi-na aji-dane.** 不思議な味だね。
It's OK/so-so.	**Mā-mā.** まあまあ。

These two are also polite ways of saying you don't really like something. The following three phrases are also handy, but best left for eating out, where you won't be insulting anyone by criticizing the food!

It's not very good.	**Anmari oishiku-nai.** あんまりおいしくない。

あんまり can be used as a softener when making a negative comment.

It doesn't taste good.	**Oishiku-nai.** おいしくない。
It's awful.	**Mazui.** まずい。 **Hidoi.** ひどい。

I can't eat this!   Kon'na-mono tabe-renai-
yo!
こんなもの食べれないよ!

This should only be used amongst friends who know you well, or you might offend your guest!

I can't believe people eat horse meat!   Basashi taberu nante
shinji-rarenai.
馬刺食べるなんて、信じられ
ない。

Basashi is raw horse meat, like sashimi 刺身.

Just try it!   Tabete-mina-yo!
食べてみなよ!

Just try a bite.   Hitokuchi dake-demo
tabete-mina-yo.
一口だけでも食べてみなよ。

It's good, I promise.   Zettai oishii kara.
絶対おいしいから。

You'll love it.   Zettai kiniiru yo.
絶対気に入るよ。

Yuck!   Oeh!
おえっ!

This is an onomatopoeia for vomiting.

I'm full.   Onaka(-ga) ippai.
お腹(が)いっぱい。
Gochisōsama(-deshita)!
ごちそうさま(でした)!

This is the end-of-meal counterpart to **itadakimas**. It literally means "it was a feast," and is a sign of appreciation.

Do you smoke?	**Tabako su'u?** タバコ吸う？
Let's get a seat in the smoking section.	**Kitsuen-seki-ni suwarō.** 喫煙席に座ろう。
This is a nonsmoking section.	**Koko-wa kin'en-seki-dayo.** ここは禁煙席だよ。
Can you drink (alcohol)?	**Osake nomeru?** (お酒)飲める？

This is perhaps more common because so many Japanese people cannot physically tolerate/process alcohol. Many get the well-known "Asian Flush" after only one drink. Before going in on a 飲み放題 **nomihōdai** (or all-you-can-drink) with people you just met, it's a good idea to make sure everyone can drink, or if not, is happy paying for an all-you-can-drink while sticking to non-alcoholic beverages. All-you-can-drinks start at around 1,000 yen for a 2-hour session if tacked onto a course-meal plan. If you're planning on having more than 3 drinks, it's usually a good idea to go with the 飲み放題 .

Do you drink beer/ saké/wine/strong liquor?	**Bīru/nihon-shu/wain/ tsuyoi osake nomu?** ビール／日本酒／ワイン／ 強いお酒飲む？

Osake means both "alcohol" and "saké." As a first question, it'll usually mean just "alcohol," but after that, it's better to say **nihonshu** which means only "saké."

Common 居酒屋 izakaya (or Japanese-style pub)
Alcoholic Beverages

beer	bīru ビール
draft beer	nama 生
mug, a medium sized one being 334ml	jokki ジョッキ
bottled beer, a medium sized bottle is 500ml	botoru ボトル
I guess I'll start with a beer.	Toriaezu bīru de. とりあえずビールで。

This is a very common phrase that people say when being asked what their first drink will be. Unlike in the States, in Japan usually people start off with a beer to kampai 乾杯! Cheers!

wine	wa-in ワイン
white wine	shiro wa-in 白ワイン
red wine	aka wa-in 赤ワイン
shōchu	sho-chū 焼酎
"sour"	sawā サワー
cocktail	kakuteru カクテル
spritzer	supuritzā スプリッツァー
Korean unfiltered rice wine	makkori マッコリ

Korean food is very popular in Japan, and many chain-izakayas carry Korean rice wine on their menu.

Shōchu mixed with hot water	oyu-wari お湯割り
sake	nihon-shu 日本酒

high ball (whiskey/soda water with lemon)	**hai-bōru** ハイボール
plum wine	**ume-shu** 梅酒

On the rocks, please.	Rokku de. ロックで。
Neat, please.	Sutoreto de. ストレートで。
Mixed with soda water, please.	Sōda-wari de. ソーダ割りで。
Mixed with water please.	Mizu-wari de. 水割りで。

If you want it mixed with warm water, you have to say: お湯割り oyu-wari.

What kinds of mixers do you have?	Nan-de watte morae-mas-ka? 何で割ってもらえますか？
Do you have cranberry juice?	Kuranberī jūsutte arimasu? クランベリージュースってあり+ ます？
Can I also have a glass of water?	Omizu mō hitotsu onegai shimasu. お水もう一つお願いします。

The Japanese don't usually drink water while they drink alcohol, and the server won't bring it unless you ask. If you want to drink and not get drunk, make sure you ask every time they bring a round of drinks!

The fountain drink machine is over there.	Asoko-ni, furī-dorinku-ga aru-yo. あそこに、フリードリンクがあるよ。
Can we buy beer here?	Koko-de bīru kaeru? ここでビール買える?
What is this, yuck!	Nani kore, mazu! 何これ、まず!
The drinks here taste terrible!	Koko-no nomimono saiaku! ここの飲み物最悪! Koko-no nomimono saiaku-dayo! ここの飲み物最悪だよ!
This is not very strong.	Kore usui/anmari koku-nai/tsuyoku-nai. これ薄い/あんまり濃くない/強くない。
They serve weak drinks here.	Koko-no nomimono zembu usui. ここの飲み物全部薄い。
Ask for stronger drinks.	Motto koi nomimono-o tanonde. もっと濃い飲み物を頼んで。
The same, but stronger.	Onaji-no-o koku-suru-yō-ni itte. 同じのを濃くするように言って。

Telling your friend to order another drink just like you have, only stronger.

Stronger drinks, please.	**Motto tsuyoi nomimono-o kudasai.** もっと強い飲み物を下さい。

When ordering the next round of drinks.

Please make this drink stronger.	**Kore motto tsuyoku/ koku-shite kudasai.** これもっと強く／濃くして下さい。

When asking the bartender to strengthen a drink you're not happy with.

Chug! Chug!	**Ikki! Ikki!** イッキ！イッキ！

Ikki! Ikki! is an encouraging cheer which means something like "Drink it all up without stopping!"

Cheers!	**Kampai!** 乾杯！

Kampai! is said together as everyone clinks their glasses for a toast. It literally means "dry glass."

Let's start with some drinks.	Toriaezu nomō. とりあえず飲もう。
I'm getting drunk.	Yotte-kichatta. 酔ってきちゃった。
	Yopparatte-kichatta. 酔っ払ってきちゃった。
	Yotte-kichatta-yo. 酔ってきちゃったよ。

All of the phrases are now gender-neutral

I'm drunk.	Yotchatta. 酔っちゃった。
	Yopparatchatta. 酔っ払っちゃった。
Let's split the check (bill).	Warikan-ni shiyō. 割り勘にしよう。
Let's pay for everything together.	Okaikei issho-ni shiyō. お会計一緒にしよう。
One check (bill), please.	Dempyō/shiharai-o hitotsu-ni shite kudasai. 伝票／支払いをひとつにして さい。

Some chain restaurants and bars also take electronic money cards, such as Suica or Waon. You can top up Suica with money at train stations or online, and Waon cards online as well. They are convenient and easy to use, and can be used at all convenience stores.

| **Which credit cards do you accept?** | **Dono kurejitto-kādo-ga tsukae-mas-ka?** どのクレジットカードが使えますか？ |

You'll find that many (especially small) shops and restaurants in Japan don't take credit cards. This is because Japan is still a mainly cash-based economy. Though ATMs are common (for withdrawing cash and transferring money) in convenience stores, there's little point-of-sale use of cash cards and virtually no checks. People generally use cash for small purchases and bank transfers for larger ones.

| **I lost my wallet.** | **Saifu-o nakushita.** 財布をなくした。 |
| | **Osaifu nakushi-chatta.** ♀ お財布なくしちゃった。 |

| **No kidding!** | **Uso!** うそ！ |

| **Are you serious?** | **Maji-de?** マジで？ |

| **That sucks!/ That's awesome!** | **Yabai-ne!** ヤバいね！ |

Yabai-ne ヤバいね (slang) is a word used to mean everything from "awesome" to "terrible" depending on the context.

| **I don't have any money.** | **Okane-ga nai.** お金がない。 |

Can I borrow 10,000 yen?

Ichiman-en kashite-kureru?
一万円借してくれる？

I've got a hangover.

Futsukayoi.
二日酔い。

I have a splitting headache.

Atama-ga suggoku itai.
頭がすっごく痛い。

You drank too much last night, huh?

Kinō nomisugitan-desho? ♀
昨日飲み過ぎたんでしょ？

Kinō nomisugitan-daro? ♂
昨日飲み過ぎたんだろ？

4

Clubbing

Let's go to a club.

Kurabu-ni ikō.
クラブに行こう。

Let's go to your favorite club.

Anata-no yoku iku kurabu-ni ikō. ♀
あなたのよく行くクラブに行こう。

Kimi-no yoku iku kurabu-ni ikō-yo. ♂
君のよく行くクラブに行こうよ。

Use **yoku iku** to describe a place you go to often.

I've never been to a club.

Mada kurabu-ni itta-koto-nai.
まだクラブに行ったことない。

Many seedy places are run by the **yakuza** (Japanese mob), and they're not to be messed with! Burly bouncers with bad attitudes are a good indicator of a **yakuza** place—until you know how things work, it's safer to stick to mainstream clubs and/or go with Japanese friends!

Is it true Japanese boys dance together?

Nihon-no otoko-no-hitotte otoko-dōshi-de odorutte hontō?
日本の男の人って男同士で踊るって本当?

How much is the cover?

Hairu-no ikura kakaru-no?
入るのいくら掛かるの?

Does it include food [and drink]?

Tabemono-toka zembu komi?
食べ物とか全部込み?

Do we need to become members?

Koko-wa membā-sei nan-des-ka?
ここはメンバー制なんですか?

Do we get membership cards?

Membāshippu/Membāzu kādo-wa morae-mas-ka?
メンバーシップ／メンバーズカードはもらえますか?

Said to club staff. When talking to friends, use the less formal **moraeru?** もらえる?

Let's make a line. (Let's get in line.)

Narabō.
並ぼう。

Are you waiting in line?

Naranderun-des-ka?
並んでるんですか?

Naranderu-no?
並んでるの?

You wait here.

Koko-de matte.
ここで待って。

I'll do it.

Atashi-ga suru-yo. ♀
あたしがするよ。

Boku-ga suru-yo. ♂
僕がするよ。

I'm a member.

Atashi-wa membā (desu). ♀
あたしはメンバー（です）。

Boku-wa membā (desu). ♂
僕はメンバー（です）。

Here are your tickets.

Hai, chiketto.
はい、チケット。

Are there lockers here?

Rokkā arimas-ka?
ロッカーありますか？

Rokkā aru?
ロッカーある？

Short-term storage lockers are common in Japan, in clubs and especially in railway stations.

Let's use the lockers.

Rokkā-(o) tsukaō.
ロッカー（を）使おう。

Where do you want to sit?

Doko-ni suwaritai?
どこに座りたい？

Let's sit close to the dance floor/bar/band/ restrooms/exit/aisle.

Dansu furoa/bā/bando/ toire/deguchi/tsūro-no chikaku-ni suwarō.

ダンスフロア／バー／バンド／トイレ／出口／通路の近く座ろう。

It's noisy here.	Koko urusaku-nai? ここうるさくない？
It's too noisy here.	Koko urusasugiru-yo-ne. ここうるさ過ぎるよね。
There are too many people here.	Hito-ōi-yo-ne. 人多いよね。 Konderu-yo-ne. 混でるよね。
It's dark over there	Mukō/Atchi kurai-yo-ne? 向こう／あっち暗いよね？
These seats look good.	Kono isu ii-yo-ne. この椅子いいよね。
Let's move to a bigger table.	Motto ōkii tēburu-ni utsurō. もっと大きいテーブルに移ろう。
We need another chair.	Mō hitotsu isu-ga iru. もうひとつ椅子が要る。
I'll get that one over there.	Are motte-kuru. あれ持って来る。
I'll bring it with me.	Motteku. 持ってく。

You sit here.	Koko-ni suwatte. ここに座って。
I'll sit here.	Koko-ni suwaru. ここに座る。
Sit by me.	Atashi-no soba/yoko-ni suwatte. ♀ あたしのそば／横に座って。 Boku-no soba/yoko-ni suwatte. ♂ 僕のそば／横に座って。

Soba means "close" and **yoko** means "beside."

Sit closer.	Motto chikaku-ni suwatte. もっと近くに座って。
Is it okay if I get drunk?	Yopparatte-mo iikana? 酔っぱらってもいいかな?
Will you dance with me?	Atashi-to odotte-kureru? ♀ あたしと踊ってくれる? Boku-to odotte-kureru? ♂ 僕と踊ってくれる? Issho-ni odoranai? 一緒に踊らない?
Let's dance!	Odorō! 踊ろう!
I can't dance	Odorenai... 踊れない...

I like to watch you dance.	Anata-no dansu-o miru-no-ga suki. ♀ あなたのダンスを見るが好き。 Kimi-no dansu-o miru-no-ga suki. ♂ 君のダンスを見るのが好き。
I'm not good at dancing.	Dansu umaku-nai-no. ♀ ダンスうまくないの。 Dansu umaku-nain-da. ♂ ダンスうまくないんだ。
Are you having fun?	Tanoshinderu? 楽しんでる？
Yes!	Un! うん！ Sō-yo! ♀ そうよ！
Not really.	Anmari. あんまり。 Betsu-ni. 別に。
I don't feel like dancing yet.	Mada odori-taku-nai. まだ踊りたくない。
I'm not going to dance yet.	Mada odoranai. まだ踊らない。

I can't dance to this music.
Kono kyoku-ja odorenai.
この曲じゃ踊れない。

I don't know this song.
Kono uta shiranai.
この歌知らない。

I like rock music.
Rokku-ga suki.
ロックが好き。

I like jazz.
Jazu-ga suki.
ジャズが好き。

I like American Top-40.
Amerikan toppu-fōtī-no ongaku/kyoku-ga suki.
アメリカントップフォーティーの音楽／曲が好き。

I like Japanese pop music.
Jei-poppu-ga suki.
ジェイ・ポップが好き。

The dance-floor lights are cool.
Furoa-no raito kakkoii-ne.
フロアのライトかっこいいね。
Furoa-no raito kakkoii-na. ♂
フロアのライトかっこいいな。

I'm getting hot.
Atsuku-natte kichatta.
暑くなって来ちゃった。

Do you want to step outside?
Chotto soto deyokka?
ちょっと外出よっか？

**Let's get some
fresh air.**

Chotto soto ikō.
ちょっと外行こう。

**What time do they
close?**

Nanji-ni shimaru-no?
何時に閉まるの？

When's the last train?

Shūden nanji?
終電何時？

Shūden 終電 is short for saishū densha 最終電車。

**What time do you
have to be at work?**

Shigoto nanji kara?
仕事何時から？

**What time is your
curfew?**

Mongen nanji?
門限何時？

We'll never make it.

Zettai mani-awanai.
絶対間に合わない。

It's already too late.

Mō osoi.
もう遅い。

We've got time.

Jikan-wa aru.
時間はある。

Let's stay to the end.

Saigo/owari-made iyō.
最後／終わりまでいよう。

**Let's stay till they
throw us out.**

Oidasareru-made iyō.
追い出されるまでいよう。

Don't you feel like eating some ramen?
Ramen tabe-taku nai?
ラーメン食べたくない？

Ramen is a very popular late-night snack in Japan, because many places are open 24 hours. Hitting a ramen joint after clubbing or heavy drinking is very common, and referred to as the しめ **shime**, or "finish."

Let's go to a café later.
Ato-de kafe-e ikō.
後でカフェへこう。

May I see you again?
Mata aeru?
また会える？

Let's exchange email addresses.
Meado kōkan shiyō.
メアド交換しよう。

Do you use Line/ Facebook?
Rain/Feisubukku yatteru?
ライン／フェイスブックやってる？

Let's hang out again.
Mata asobō-yo.
また遊ぼうよ。

I know an even better place (than here).
Motto ii-toko shitteru-kara.
もっと良いとこ知ってるから。

5

Sweet Talk

Although Japan is still a relatively patriarchal society, younger women are becoming more forward when it comes to romance. It's not unusual to hear of girls making the first move, or asking a guy out on a date. Girls still "act cute" **kawai-ko-buru** かわいこぶる in front of guys, but are not as hesitant about making their intentions known as in older generations. Don't be surprised if girls try to **gyaku-nan** 逆ナン、or pick-up guys.

Guys and girls tend to say **nandemo ii-yo** 何でもいいよ, or "It doesn't matter/I don't care/You can decide." It's less of a gender thing than it is a cultural one. It's common to **awaseru** 合せる, or go with the majority's wishes, such as ordering beer as the first drink (refer to Chapter 3 Eating and Drinking)

| **I had a great time yesterday/last night/last week/last Friday.** | Kinō/Kinō-no yoru/Senshū/ Senshū-no kin-yōbi-wa tanoshi-katta. 昨日／昨日の夜／先週／ 先週 の金曜日は楽しかった。 |

Do you think of me often?

Atashi-no-koto yoku kangaeru? ♀
あたしのことよく考える?

Boku-no-koto yoku kangaeru? ♂
僕のことよく考える?

I think of you night and day.

Anata-no-koto ichinichi-jū kangaeteru. ♀
あなたのこと一日中考えてる。

Kimi-no-koto ichinichi-jū kangaeteru-yo. ♂
君の事一日中考えてるよ。

I couldn't stop thinking about you.

Anata-no-koto bakkari kangaeteta. ♀
あなたのことばっかり考えてた。

Kimi-no-koto bakkari kangaeteta. ♂
君のことばっかりえ考てた。

I remember what you said.

Anata-ga itta-koto oboeteru. ♀
あなたが言ったこと覚えてる。

Kimi-ga itta-koto oboeteru. ♂
君が言ったこと覚えてる。

For "remembered," change **oboeteru** to **oboeteta** 覚えてた. To turn the conversation back to what was said (and to sound even more interested!), try using a rising intonation with these two phrases.

I wanted to call you sooner.	Motto hayaku denwa shita-katta. もっと早く電話したかった。
What would you like to do tonight?	Kon-ya nani shitai? 今夜何したい？
What sounds good?	Dō-shiyō-ka? どうしようか？

Dō-shiyō-ka? is a classic case illustrating the vital role of pronunciation. With a rising intonation (and preferably also an interested tone), it means "What sounds good?" But with a flat intonation and a concerned tone, it means "Now what the hell are we going to do?" as when you've got a big problem on your hands.

The boy should make the decision so he doesn't seem weak. The girl will most likely say **Wakan'nai** 分かんない ("I don't know/care"); **Makaseru-wa!** 任せるわ ("It's up to you"—the boy's equivalent is **Makaseru-yo** 任せるよ); or **Kimete** 決めて ("You decide").

Do you cook often?	Yoku ryōri suru? よく料理する？
We could cook dinner together.	Issho-ni gohan tsukurō-ka? 一緒にご飯作ろうか？
I'd like to try your home cooking.	Anata-no teryōri-ga tabetai. ♀ あなたの手料理が食べたい。 Kimi-no teryōri-ga tabetai. ♂ 君の手料理が食べたい。

What's your best dish?   Tokui-ryōri-wa nani?
得意料理は何？

I want to try that.   Sore tabete-mitai.
それ食べてみたい。

**Can we meet
tomorrow?**   Ashita aeru?
明日あえる？

**Can you go out this
Saturday?**   Kondo-no doyōbi
derareru?
今度の土曜日出られる？

This means "Can you get out of the house this Saturday?"
Use ...dekakerareru? 出かけられる？ for "Can you go out
with me...?"

I can't wait!   Tanoshimi!
楽しみ！

Closer in meaning to "I'm looking forward to it!"

I can wait till then.   Sore-made materu.
それまで待てる。
Matsu-wa. ♀
待つわ。
Matsu-yo. ♂
待つよ。

**I like holding your
hand.**   Anata-to te-o tsunagu-
no-ga suki. ♀
あなたと手をつなぐのが好き。
Kimi-to te-o tsunagu-no-ga
suki. ♂
君と手をつなぐのが好き。

Kiss me.	Kisu shite. キスして。
French kiss me.	Shita irete. 舌入れて。
Use your tongue.	Shita tsukatte. 舌使って。
Kiss me deeply.	Oishii kisu shite. おいしいキスして。

This is another use of "**oishii**"—see Chapter 3 Eating and Drinking. The Japanese almost always translate **oishii** as "delicious"—an appropriate image here!

I like kissing you.	Anata-to kisu suru-no suki. ♀ あなたとキスするの好き。 Kimi-to kisu suru-no suki. ♂ 君とキスするの好き。

Girls use **anata** あなた to mean "you" when speaking, especially to a significant other, and men use **omae/kimi** お前／君 when speaking to women. Older generations call to their spouses in this way. It is very rarely used in day-to-day conversations, especially in public, though. It is more common to say their name when talking to them. So you can say: **Tarō-no kuchibiru yawarakai** 「太郎の唇やわらかい」 ("Taro's lips are soft") when you're kissing Taro.

You're a good kisser.	Kisu-ga jōzu. キスが上手。

Your lips are so soft.	(anata no kuchibiru) yawarakai. (あなたの唇)柔らかい。

The object can be inferred through context.

You're the only one I want.	Atashi-ga hoshii-no-wa anata-dake. ♀ あたしが欲しいのはあなただけ。 Boku-ga hoshii-no-wa kimi-dake. ♂ 僕が欲しいのは君だけ。
There's something I want to tell you.	Sugoku hanashitai koto-ga aru-no. ♀ すごく話したい事があるの。 Sugoku hanashitai koto-ga arun-da-kedo. すごく話したい事があるんだけど。

Use this to show your excitement/enthusiasm just before saying what's on your mind, inviting your friend to ask **Nani? Nani?** 何？何？ "What?"

I'm really excited/ nervous right now.	Ima suggoku doki-doki shiteru-yo. 今すっごくどきどきしてるよ。
It's like/feels like a dream.	Yume mitai. 夢みたい。
I'm so happy right now.	Ima sugoku shiawase. 今すごく幸せ。

Stay here/don't leave.

Koko-ni ite.
ここにいて。

I can't think of anything but you.

Anata-no-koto igai-wa kangae-rarenai. ♀
あなたの事以外は考えられない。

Kimi-no-koto igai-wa kangae-rarenai. ♂
君の事以外は考えられない。

I can't live without you(r love).

Anata-nashi-ja iki-rarenai. ♀
あなた無しじゃ生きられない。

Kimi-nashi-ja iki-rarenai. ♂
君無しじゃ生きられない。

It hurts to be without you.

Anata-nashi-da-to tsurai. ♀
あなた無しだとつらい。

Kimi-nashi-da-to tsurai. ♂
君無しだとつらい。

Say you'll be mine.

Atashi-no mono-to itte. ♀
あたしのものと言って。

Boku-no mono-to itte. ♂
僕のものと言って。

I'll make you happy.

Shiawase-ni suru-yo. ♂
幸せにするよ。

Girls might take this as a proposal.

I've never felt this way before.

Kon'na kimochi hajimete.
こんな気持ち初めて。

That was fun, huh?	Tanoshi-katta-ne? 楽しかったね? Tanoshi-katta-na? ♂ 楽しかったな?
I liked you from the moment I saw you.	Hajimete atta toki-kara iinatte omotteta. 初めてあった時からいいなって思ってた。
You're special (to me).	Anata-wa tokubetsu-yo. ♀ あなたは特別よ。 Kimi-wa tokubetsu-dayo. ♂ 君は特別だよ。
I like you a lot/ I love you.	Dai-suki. 大好き。

Suki means "like," and you can add **dai** to mean literally "more like" or "bigger like" to express deeper feelings. 愛してる is only used in private, between lovers, never family.

I want to be closer to you.	Motto chikaku-ni kite. もっと近くに来て。
Hold my hand.	Te-o nigitte. 手を握って。
Don't leave.	Kaeranai-de. 帰らないで。

What do you think about me?

Watashi/boku-no-koto dō omotteru? ♀ / ♂
私／僕のことどう思ってる？

Do you remember our first date?

Hajimete-no dēto oboeteru?
初めてのデート覚えてる？

Look into my eyes.

Atashi-no me-o mite. ♀
あたしの目を見て。

Boku-no me-o mite. ♂
僕の目を見て。

Stay just a little bit longer.

Mō chotto-dake issho-ni-iyō.
もうちょっとだけ一緒にいよう。

I couldn't have done it without you.

Anata-nashi-ja dekina-katta. ♀
あなた無しじゃできなかった。

Kimi-nashi-ja dekina-katta. ♂
君無しじゃできなかった。

Stay with me tonight.

Konya-wa atashi-to issho-ni ite. ♀
今夜はあたしと一緒にいて。

Konya-wa boku-to issho-ni ite. ♂
今夜は僕と一緒にいて。

I'll tell you something—I love you.

Chotto kiite, (anata-ga) suki.
ちょっと聞いて、（あなたが）好き。

Chotto kiite, suki-dayo. ♂
ちょっと聞いて、好きだよ。

Saying "love" in Japanese can be a bit tricky. **Ai** (愛) is the direct translation of "love," but it's generally only for movie titles or as a joke. In normal conversation, you usually say **suki** (好き) and convey the feeling of love by the emotion and emphasis in your voice.

I know what's on your mind.	**Anata-ga nani kangaeteru-ka shitteru.** ♀ あなたが何 考 えてるか知ってる。 **Kimi-ga nani kangaeteru-ka shitteru-yo.** ♂ 君が何 考 えてるか知ってるよ。
No, you don't.	**Wakaruwakenai-deshō.** ♀ 分る訳ないでしょう。 **Wakaruwakenai-darō.** ♂ 分る訳ないだろう。
You're thinking dirty thoughts.	**Anata-wa yarashii-koto kangaeteru deshō.** ♀ あなたはやらしいこと 考 えてるでしょう。 **Kimi-wa yarashii-koto kangaeterun-ja nai-no?** ♂ 君はやらしいこと 考 えてるんじゃないの？
So are you.	**Anata-mo.** ♀ あなたも。 **Kimi-mo.** ♂ 君も。

I like that kind of thinking.	Sō-iu kangae suki. そういう考え好き。
You're the only one I love.	Suki-nano-wa anata-dake. ♀ 好きなのはあなただけ。 Suki-nano-wa kimi-dake. ♂ 好きなのは君だけ。

Go easy (at first) on the sweet talk. Japanese boys don't throw around a lot of compliments or terms of endearment, so most girls are not accustomed to such attention. However, in the long run, most will definitely enjoy it.

I don't love anyone else.	Hoka-no dare-mo suki-janai. 他の誰も好きじゃない。
I love you so much I could die.	Shinu-hodo suki. 死ぬほど好き。
I love you just the way you are.	Sonomama-no anata-ga suki. ♀ そのままのあなたが好き。 Sonomama-no kimi-ga suki. ♂ そのままの君が好き。
Now is the right time.	Ima-ga sono-toki-yo. ♀ 今がその時よ。 Ima-ga sono-toki-dayo. ♂ 今がその時だよ。

Hold me tight.	Shikkari dakishimete. ♀ しっかり抱き締めて。 Tsuyoku dakishimete. ♂ 強く抱き締めて。
Be with me tonight.	Kon'ya-wa issho-ni ite. 今夜は一緒にいて。
I don't want to go home tonight.	Kon'ya-wa uchi-ni kaeri-taku-nai. ♀ 今夜は家に帰りたくない。

A popular phrase. If she says this, pat yourself on the back.

Do you want to come to my place?	Uchi-ni kuru? 家に来る？
I don't want to be used.	Asobare-taku-nai. 遊ばれたくない。

Asobu 遊ぶ means "to play." This passive form literally means "to be played/mucked around with."

Believe in me. (Trust me.)	Atashi-o shinjite. ♀ あたしを信じて。 Boku-o shinjite. ♂ 僕を信じて。
I want to know all about you.	Anata-no-koto subete shiritai. ♀ あなたのこと全て知りたい。 Kimi-no-koto subete shiritai. ♂ 君のこと全て知りたい。

You mean so much to me.	**Anata-wa tottemo taisetsu-na hito-yo.** ♀ あなたはとっても大切な人よ。 **Kimi-wa tottemo taisetsu-na hito-nan-da.** ♂ 君はとっても大切な人なんだ。

This is a very powerful expression of love and devotion. Use with caution.

I want to make love to you.	**Aishi-aitai.** 愛し合いたい。

Make love to me.	**Daite.** ♀ 抱いて。

Younger people use the loan word **sekkusu** セックス for "sex." So you can say **sekkusu shitai** セックスしたい ("I want to have sex (with you)"), but girls find this a little too straightforward, and prefer a more subtle expression of passion, like the one above. Men may want to say this with their friends if they're all in the mood (and not getting any).

6

Making Love

It's too early (to go to bed).	Mada hayai. まだ早い。 Etchi shiyō. エッチしよう。 Etchi suru? エッチする？ Etchi shitai-nā. エッチしたいなあ。

Japanese do not often directly say "Let's go to bed." Instead the words are conveyed by the mood. These phrases are useful in case you miss the mood signals.

Let's go to a love hotel.	Rabuho ikō-ka. ♂ ラブホ行こうか。

Rabuho ラブホ is short for **Rabu-hoteru** ラブホテル。

Young Japanese usually live with their parents right up to their wedding day. With small houses or apartments and paper-thin walls, the living arrangements are not conducive to good sex. Owning a car provides little escape, for there are few pleasant, obscure places to park short of driving two or three hours to the countryside. So, where do the non-farmers go for a roll in the hay? Have you heard of a love hotel? No? Then step this way...

Identifying a love hotel is easy, as most of them are near big train stations (four tracks or more), in entertainment districts, and along major highways.

They are usually well-lit with colorful Japanese characters or **rōmaji** in neon, or just a sign saying "Hotel," with some twinkling stars floating around it. If there are no obvious markings, look for big, big objects on the roof. A 30-foot mock Statue of Liberty or Queen Elizabeth (the ship, that is) on top of a building that has no other visible ads or signs is a dead giveaway. Also, the absence of a doorman and a lobby with a front desk should scream love hotel.

The service at a love hotel is very discreet; you don't see them and they don't see you. ID's aren't even checked, as there's a rule of thumb: if you're old enough to pay, you're old enough to play.

Come over here/ **Come closer to me.**	Motto kocchi oide-yo/ Motto soba-ni kite. もっとこっちおいでよ。／ もっとそばに来て。
I'm so glad we waited.	Matte yokatta. 待って良かった。
Don't tease me.	Jirasanai-de. ♀ じらさないで。 Jirasuna-yo. ♂ じらすなよ。

(You) smell good.　　Ii nioi.
良い匂い。

I like how you smell.　Anata/kimi-no nioi
suki-dayo. ♀ / ♂
あなた／君のにおい好きだよ。

**Your skin is so soft/
smooth.**　(Hada sugoi) sube-sube.
(肌すごい)すべすべ。

If you say this while touching the person's skin, there is no
need to specify what is **sube-sube** すべすべ。

What perfume/cologne　Nan-no kōsui/koron
are you wearing?　tsuketeru-no?
何の香水／コロンつけてるの?

What color underwear　(Kyō) Nani iro-no shitagi
are you wearing　tsuketeru-no?
(today)?　(今日)何色の下着つけてるの?

I like your underwear.　Sono shitagi kawaii-ne.
その下着かわいいね。

Sono shitagi kawaii-na. ♂
その下着かわいいな。

Kawaii literally means "cute."

That tickles.　Kusuguttai.
くすぐったい。

Kusuguttai-yo. ♂
くすぐったいよ。

You have beautiful　Hada kirei-dane. ♂
skin.　肌きれいだね。

I found your birthmark.	Koko-ni hokuro-o mitsuketa. ここにほくろを見つけた。
I'm getting excited.	Waku-waku shite-kichatta. わくわくしてきちゃった。
Will you use a condom?	Gomu tsukete. ♀ ゴムつけて。
I'll use a condom.	Gomu tsukeru. ♂ ゴムつける。
I forgot to bring a condom.	Kondōmu/gomu motte nai-yo. コンドーム／ゴム持ってないよ。

コンドーム is the loan word for "condom," ゴム means "rubber."

Don't worry, I'm on the pill.	Piru nonderu-kara daijōbu. ピル飲んでるから大丈夫。
I'm not on the pill.	Piru nonde-nai. ピル飲んでない。

The pill is still not nearly as commonplace as a method of birth control in Japan. A lot of women are afraid of the side effects (weight gain, hormonal changes, etc.), and do not have a lot of practical knowledge about birth control methods besides condoms. Unless the girl has spent time abroad or is a sexually open person, it's safe to assume she isn't on the pill.

I don't want to use a condom.	Gomu tsuke-taku-nai. ゴムつけたくない。
We're not having sex unless we use a condom.	Tsuke-nai nara yara-nai. つけないならヤラない。
Could you go buy some?	Katte-kite? 買ってきて?
Have you been tested since your last partner?	Saigo-ni sekkusu shita ato, kensa shita? 最後にセックスした後、検査した?

This is a very sensitive subject in Japan also, but people don't talk about it as openly with their sexual partners as they might in more sexually open cultures. If your partner has had many partners, it might be a good idea to ask. STD tests are usually not covered by insurance, and can range between 3,000 yen to 20,000 yen, depending on what you get tested for and where.

I've never been tested.	Kensa shita-koto-nai. 検査したことない。
Yeah I did, and I'm fine/disease-free.	Un, demo daijōbu-datta. うん、でも大丈夫だった。
I was tested positive two years ago, but I haven't had any symptoms for the past year.	Ninen-mae-ni yōsei datta-kedo, mō ichinen shōjō-wa dete-nai. 二年前に陽性だったけど、もう一年症状はでてない。

Then we have to make sure to use a condom.	Jā, chanto kondōmu tsukawanakya. じゃあ、ちゃんとコンドーム使わなきゃ。
When was your first experience?	Saisho-ni shita-no-wa itsu? 最初にしたのはいつ？
Where was your first experience?	Saisho doko-de shita? 最初どこでした？
I did it at ...	...-de shita-no. ♀ …でしたの。 ...-de shita. ♂ …でした。
I won't tell you.	Oshiete-agenai. ♀ 教えてあげない。 Oshienai. 教えない。
I forgot.	Wasure-chatta. 忘れちゃった。 Wasureta-yo. 忘れたよ。
Actually, you're my first.	Jitsu-wa anata-ga hajimete-nano. ♀ 実はあなたが初めてなの。 Jitsu-wa kimi-ga hajimete-nanda. ♂ 実は君が初めてなんだ。

I'm a virgin.	**Shojo-nano.** ♀ 処女なの。 **Dōtei-nanda.** ♂ 童貞なんだ。
Do you like to do it in the shower/bath?	**Shawā/Ofuro-de suru-no-ga suki?** シャワー／お風呂でするのが好き？
Do you like to do it in the morning?	**Asa suru-no-ga suki?** 朝するのが好き？
Do you like to do it in the morning or at night?	**Asa-ha? Yoru-ha?** 朝派？夜派？
I think I prefer morning sex.	**Asa-no-hō-ga suki-kamo.** 朝の方が好きかも。
Have you ever had anal sex?	**Anaru sekkusu shita-koto aru?** アナルセックスしたことある？
Yes I have.	**Shita-koto aru.** したことある。
Never.	**Shita-koto nai.** したことない。
No...oo/Gross...s. (elongated for playfulness)	**Yadā.** やだぁ。

Absolutely not!
(very serious)

Zettai yada!
絶対やだ！

Sounds fun.

Omoshirosō.
面白そう。

Is it gonna hurt?

Itai-kana?
痛いかな？

Do you do it by yourself/
Do you masturbate?

Hitori-de-wa?
一人では？

How many sexual
partners have you had?

Kore-made-ni nan-nin-to
neta-koto ga aru?/Sekkusu
shita?
これまでに何人と寝たことが
ある？／セックスした？

Do you masturate?

Onanī suru?
オナニーする？

Just joking.

Uso/Jōdan-dayo.
嘘／冗談だよ。

Buttocks

oshiri
おしり

ketsu ♂
けつ

Thigh

momo
股

Waist

koshi
腰

There is no word for "hips" in Japanese—**koshi** is as close as it gets.

Belly button	**oheso** おへそ
Breast(s)	**oppai** おっぱい **mune** 胸
Nipple(s)	**chikubi** ちくび
Ear lobe	**mimitabu** 耳たぶ
Nape of the neck	**unaji** うなじ

Japanese men find this especially erotic.

Down there	**asoko** あそこ

Asoko usually means "over there" but in this sense it means the "private parts."

Bush	**asoko-no ke** ♂ あそこの毛

As above, this means "the hair down there."

Cunt	**omanko** ♂ おまんこ **omeko** ♂ おめこ

Omanko is used in the Kantō (greater Tōkyō) area, and **omeko** is preferred in the Kansai (greater Ōsaka).

Touch me here.	Koko sawatte. ここ触って。

You can say this while guiding their hand.

Pubic hair (can be used for men or women)	asoko-no ke あそこの毛
cunt/pussy/vulva	omanko おまんこ
penis	penisu ペニス
"my son"	musuko ムスコ
testicles/balls	kintama 金玉

Literally, "balls of gold"!

Cock	chinchin ちんちん
Hard-on	chinchin-ga tatsu ♂ ちんちんがたつ bokki suru ♂ ぼっきする
(I'm/you're) wet.	Nureteru. ぬれてる。

Depends on the context/who's talking.

I'm getting really excited/turned on.	**Kōfun suru.** 興奮する。
pre-cum	**gaman-jiru** 我慢汁
to come/ "I'm going to come"	**iku** イク
To come	**gaman-jiru** ♂ 我慢汁 **seishi** 精子

Gaman-jiru is more like the preliminary shot before the ecstatic blast (**seishi**).

fellatio/blow-job/ oral sex	**shabutte** ♂ しゃぶって **sakku** ♂ サック **fera** ♂ フェラ

Fera is more vulgar—if you're asking your girlfriend, it's better to say **sakku**.

balls	**kintama** 金玉

Naturally enough, the words marked for guys only are pretty vulgar, and shouldn't be used when there are girls around! And Japanese girls tend to be very vague about these parts of the body, preferring to say **asoko** and to make allusions.

Kiss my neck.	Kubi-ni kisu shite. 首にキスして。
Touch me more gently.	Motto yasashiku sawatte. もっとやさしく触って。
Be rougher with me.	Motto rafu-ni shite. もっとラフにして。
Hold on a second.	Chotto matte. ちょっと待って。
Lick my nipples.	Chikubi-o namete. ♀ ちくびをなめて。
Sixty-nine.	Shikkusu-nain. シックスナイン。

It's "six-nine" in Japanese, not "sixty-nine."

I like to "sixty-nine."	Shikkusu-nain suki. シックスナイン好き。
Let's do "sixty-nine."	Shikkusu-nain-de shiyō. シックスナインでしよう。
Show me what turns you on/stimulates you.	Doko-ga kanjiru-ka oshiete. どこが感じるか教えて。
I like to try different styles.	Chigau tai'i/pojishon de yaru-no-ga suki. 違う体位／ポジションでヤルのが好き。

Let's try a different style.	Chigau tai'i-de shiyō. 違う体位でしよう。
Think of a new position.	Atarashii tai'i-o kangaete. 新しい体位を考えて。
I'm tired of that one.	Are-wa akita. あれは飽きた。
That's original.	Kore-wa atarashii-ne. これは新しいね。
That sounds exciting.	Doki-doki shichau. どきどきしちゃう。 Doki-doki suru. どきどきする。 Waku-waku-shichau. わくわくしちゃう。 Waku-waku-suru. わくわくする。

Wakuwaku-shichau/suru can also be used in nonsexual contexts such as "That party sounds exciting."

Let's do it again.	Mō ikkai shiyō. もう一回しよう。
Missionary position/ Girl bottom/boy top	Seijōi 正常位
Boy bottom/girl top	Kijōi 騎乗位
Doggy style	Bakku バック

Kōbai
後背位
こう はい い

Seijōi literally means "normal"; **Kijōi** means "to ride"; and **bakku** means, well, you know. To express "Let's do it doggy style," one would say **Bakku shiyō**; for "Let's use the missionary position," one would say **Seijōi-de shiyō**.

Did it hurt?	Itaku-nakatta? ♂ 痛くなかった？ いた
It did!	Ita-katta! ♀ 痛かった！ いた
No, it didn't.	Itaku-nakatta(-no). ♀ 痛くなかった（の）。 いた
Do Japanese couples have car sex?	Nihon-no kappuru-wa kā-sekkusu suru-no? 日本のカップルはカーセックスするの？ に ほん
Yes, but not often.	Un, demo son'na-ni yaranai. うん、でもそんなにやらない。
No. There aren't any good places.	Uun, ii basho-ga nai. ううん、いい場所がない。 ば しょ
Where do they go?	Min'na doko-ni iku-no? みんなどこに行くの？ い
Let's find a good place.	Ii basho-o sagasō. いい場所を探そう。 ば しょ さが

How do you know of such a place?

Son'na basho nan-de shitteru-no?
そんな場所何で知ってるの？

People can see us here.

Koko-ja hito-ni miechau-yo.
ここじゃ人に見えちゃうよ。

That'll make it more exciting.

Shigeki-teki. ♀
刺激的。

Shigeki-teki-dane. ♂
刺激的だね。

Let's get in the back seat.

Bakku shīto-ni suwarō.
バックシートに座ろう。

Let's recline the front seats.

Furonto shīto-o taosō.
フロントシートを倒そう。

Let's use the blanket.

Mōfu-o tsukaō.
毛布を使おう。

The blanket's dirty.

Mōfu kitanai-nē.
毛布汚いねえ。

Take your shoes off.

Kutsu-o nugi-na-yo. ♂
靴を脱ぎなよ。

Relax.

Rirakkusu shite.
リラックスして。

Enjoy yourself.

Enjoi shite.
エンジョイして。

Take your ... off.

   Shoes

Kutsu-o nuide.
靴を脱いで。

   Bra

Burajā-o hazushite.
ブラジャーをはずして。

   Underwear

Shitagi-o totte.
下着をとって。

   Clothes

Fuku-o nuide.
服を脱いで。

I'm cold.

Samui.
寒い。

Make me warm.

Atatamete.
暖めて。

Attamete.
あっためて。

Doesn't that feel better?

Sono-hō-ga kimochi yokunai?
その方が気持ちよくない？

Do it like this.

Kon'na-fū-ni shite.
こんなふうにして。

That's right.

Sō-dane.
そうだね。

Sō-dana. ♂
そうだな。

Mā-ne.
まあね。

Māne is often used to mean "I know." If said teasingly, it means "Yeah, I know (but I might not tell you)."

| **We did it.** | Yatchatta.
やっちゃった。 |

This literally means "I did it"—you'll be clear by the context!

In Japanese there is a slang use of "A," "B," and "C" similar to the American English slang use of "first base," "second base," "third base," and "home run." These letters denote kissing, petting, and making love, respectively, so you could say **A shita** エーした etc.

| **I scored with her/She**
let me go all the way. | Yarasete kureta.
ヤラせてくれた。 |

Yara やる literally means "do."

Nampa ナンパ can also be used as a verb, which means to "pick someone up" or "hit on." A guy can brag: "I picked up a really cute girl yesterday. 昨日かわいい子ナンパしちゃったよ。 **Kinō kawaii-ko nampa shichatta-yo.**"

Recently, girls can also **nampa** ナンパ guys. In this case, you can say **gyakunan** 逆ナン (opposite of **nampa**). A guy can also brag: "I got picked up/hit on by a super cute girl last night! 昨日の夜すげーかわいい子に逆ナンされちゃってさ！ **Kinō-no-yoru sugē kawaii-ko-ni gyaku-nan sare-chatte-sa!**"

7

Oops!

I have some good news.	Ii shirase-ga aru-no. ♀ いい知らせがあるの。
We have to talk.	Hanashi-ga aru. 話がある。
I can't tell you on the phone.	Denwa-ja ie-nai. ♀ 電話じゃ言えない。
You're going to be a father!	Anata-wa papa-ni naru-no-yo! ♀ あなたはパパになるのよ！
I'm pregnant.	Atashi ninshin shiteru-no. ♀ あたし妊娠してるの。
Congratulations!	Omedetō! ♂ おめでとう！
Are you sure?	Hontō-ni? ♂ 本当に？

I haven't had my period yet.	Seiri-ga konai-no. ♀ 生理が来ないの。
When was your last period?	Saigo-no seiri-wa itsu kita-no? ♂ 最後の生理はいつ来たの？
Maybe it was too early to take the test.	Kensa-o suru-ni-wa hayasugirun-janai. ♂ 検査をするには早過ぎるんじゃない。
Take the test again.	Mō ikkai kensa shite-mite. ♂ もう一回検査してみて。
When did you find out?	Itsu wakatta-no? ♂ いつ分かったの？
Why didn't you tell me sooner?	Nan-de motto hayaku iwa-nakatta-no? ♂ 何でもっと早く言わなかったの？
I've been wanting to tell you, but (I didn't)...	Iita-katta-kedo... ♀ 言いたかったけど…。
What week are you now?	Ima nan-shū-me? ♂ 今何週目？
When's the baby due?	Yoteibi-wa itsu? ♂ 予定日はいつ？
It's going to change our lives.	Kore-kara isogashiku naru-ne. ♂ これから忙しくなるね。

Literally means "We're going to get busy from now on..."

I want a boy/girl.	Otoko-no-ko/On'na-no-ko-ga ii. 男の子／女の子がいい。
It is/was our destiny.	Kitto unmei dattan-dane. きっと運命だったんだね。
There's no better news than this.	Kore-ijō ureshii-koto-wa nai-yo. ♂ これ以上うれしい事はないよ。
When will your stomach show?	Itsu-goro-kara onaka-ga ōkiku naru-no? ♂ いつごろからお腹が大きくなるの？
Take good care of yourself.	Muri shinai yō-ni-ne. ♂ 無理しないようにね。
(We should) start reading books about babies.	Soro-soro akachan-no hon-o yomi hajime-yō-ka. ♂ そろそろ赤ちゃんの本を読み始めようか。
We should think of a name.	Namae-o kangae-nakucha. 名前を考えなくちゃ。
Are you sure it's mine?	Hontō-ni boku-no-ko? ♂ 本当に僕の子？
Why would you ask me such a thing?	Nan-de son'na-koto kiku-no? ♀ 何でそんな事聞くの？

I guess the condom broke, huh?	Chanto gomu tsuke-nakattan-dane? ちゃんとゴムつけなかったんだね。
I thought you said you used a condom!	Gomu tsuketetatte itta-jan. ♀ ゴムつけてたって言ったじゃん。
I can't be held responsible.	Boku-ni sekinin-wa nai. ♂ 僕に責任はない。
You gonna just run away from it?	Nigeru-no? 逃げるの？
This is impossible/ I can't do this.	Muri. 無理。
Take responsibility.	Sekinin totte. ♀ 責任とって。
We have to think about what we're gong to do.	Dō suru-ka chanto kangae-yō. どうするかちゃんと考えよう。

This is a useful and very "Japanese" phrase—it literally means "think about it well," but it carries the nuance of "you have to do this."

You knew it could happen, didn't you?	Kō-naru-kamo shirenai-tte wakattetan-janai-no? こうなるかもしれないって分かってたんじゃないの？

You are terrible/ unbelievable.

Saitei.
最低。

Men and women say this when they are disgusted with the person they are talking to. It usually does the trick.

See you later.

Ato-de-ne. ♀
後でね。

Ato-de-na. ♂
後でな。

Don't call me.

Denwa shinaide.
電話しないで。

I'll call you later.

Atashi-ga ato-de denwa suru. ♀
あたしが後で電話する。

Boku-ga ato-de denwa suru. ♂
僕が後で電話する。

You'll be sorry.

Kōkai suru-yo.
後悔するよ。

It's a bad time.

Taimingu-ga warui.
タイミングが悪い。

It's too early.

Hayasugiru.
早過ぎる。

It's your fault.

Anata-no-sei. ♀
あなたのせい。

Kimi-no-sei. ♂
君のせい。

Please give it up this time/let's stop arguing.	Gomen-ne, akiramete. ごめんね、あきらめて。
We have to think about it carefully.	Motto chanto kangae-nakya. もっとちゃんと考えなきゃ。
I wish it were a dream.	Yume-dattara yokatta-noni. 夢だったらよかったのに。
What will happen to us?	Atashi-tachi dō narun-darō? ♀ あたしたちどうなるんだろう？ Boku-tachi dō narun-darō? ♂ 僕たちどうなるんだろう？
What do we do now?	Dō suru? どうする？
I don't know what to do.	Dōshita-ra ii-ka wakan'nai. どうしたらいいか分かんない。
Let's decide together.	Futari-de kime-yō. 二人で決めよう。 Issho-ni kime-yō. 一緒に決めよう。 Issho-ni kangae-yō. 一緒に考えよう。
It's up to you.	Anata-ni makaseru. ♀ あなたに任せる。 Kimi-ni makaseru. ♂ 君に任せる。

You decide.

Anata-ga kimete. ♀
あなたが決めて。

Kimi-ga kimete. ♂
君が決めて。

Let me think it over.

Mō ichido kangae-sasete.
もう一度考えさせて。

Whatever you want to do will be fine with me.

Anata-ga shitai-yō-ni shite ii-wa. ♀
あなたがしたいようにしていいわ。

Kimi-ga shitai-yō-ni shite ii-yo. ♂
君がしたいようにしていいよ。

The child is ours, not just mine.

Akachan-wa atashi-dake-no-mono-janai-wa. ♀
赤ちゃんはあたしだけのものじゃないわ。

Akachan-wa boku-dake-no mono-janai-yo. ♂
赤ちゃんは僕だけのものじゃないよ。

I'm scared.

Kowai(-yo). ♀
怖い(よ)。

I want to have the baby.

Atashi-wa umitai. ♂
あたしは産みたい。

It's our baby.

Atashi-tachi-no akachan-yo. ♀
あたしたちの赤ちゃんよ。

	Boku-tachi-no akachan-dayo. ♂ 僕たちの赤ちゃんだよ。
What do you think?	Dō omou? どう思う？
Let's raise the baby (together).	(Futari-de) sodate-yō. (二人で)育てよう。
I don't need your help/ I can raise the baby by myself.	Atashi hitori-de sodateru. ♀ あたしひとりで育てる。 Boku hitori-de sodateru. ♂ 僕ひとりで育てる。
It's impossible to have a baby now.	Ima akachan-o sodateru-no-wa muri-yo. ♀ 今赤ちゃんを育てるのは無理よ。 Ima akachan-o sodateru-no-wa muri-dayo. ♂ 今赤ちゃんを育てるのは無理だよ。
We're not ready yet.	Mada hayai. まだ早い。
Let's have the operation.	Byōin-e ikō. 病院へ行こう。

This literally means "let's go to the hospital."

You're such a cold person!	Anata-tte hontō-ni tsumetai-no-ne! ♀ あなたって本当に冷たいのね！

Kimi-tte hontō-ni
tsumetai-na! ♂
君って本当に冷たいな！

I can't kill our baby. Atashi-tachi-no akachan-o
orosenai. ♀
あたしたちの赤ちゃんをおろ
せない。

Boku-tachi-no akachan-o
orosenai. ♂
僕たちの赤ちゃんをおろせない。

Abortion (中絶／chūzetsu) does have a social stigma
attached to it, but not as much, at least not religiously
based, as in Western countries. Most women don't talk
about it openly, and if they were to get one, they are basically hush-hush about it.

I'll get an abortion. Orosu-wa. ♀
おろすわ。

I don't have a choice Orosu-shika nai-yo-ne.
but to get an abortion. おろすしかないよね。

I'm scared, but I don't Kowai-kedo, shikataga-nai.
have a choice. 怖いけど、仕方がない。

There aren't any Hoka-ni sentakushi-
other options. wa nai.
他に選択肢はない。

(Don't worry), I won't (Daijōbu,) Oya-ni-wa
tell my parents. iwanai-kara.
(大丈夫、)親には言わない
から。

Don't worry.

Shimpai shinaide.
心配しないで。

My friend said she has had an abortion too.

Tomodachi-mo oroshita-koto arutte itteta.
友達もおろしたことあるって言ってた。

This is the right choice.

Kore-ga tadashii sentaku-da-to omou.
これが正しい選択だと思う。

We don't have a choice.

Son'na-koto itte-rarenai.
そんな事いってられない。

Shikata-ga-nai.
仕方がない。

I'll pay for it.

Atashi-ga harau. ♀
あたしが払う。

Boku-ga harau. ♂
僕が払う。

How much does it cost?

Ikura kakaru?
いくらかかる?

Do you have that much money?

Son'na okane motteru-no?
そんなお金持ってるの?

I don't have enough money.

Son'na-ni okane nai-yo.
そんなにお金ないよ。

I'll earn the money (for it).

Okane-o yōi suru-wa. ♀
お金を用意するわ。

Okane-o yōi suru-yo. ♂
お金を用意するよ。

I can get it.	Atsumerareru-yo. 集められるよ。
Will you go with me?	Atashi-to issho-ni kite-kureru? ♀ あたしと一緒に来てくれる？
I'll be with you.	Issho-ni iru-kara. 一緒にいるから。
It will be okay.	Daijōbu-dayo. 大丈夫だよ。
You're not alone.	Hitori janai-yo. 一人じゃないよ。
I'm not going anywhere.	Doko-ni-mo ikanai. どこにも行かない。
Do you have to stay in the hospital (overnight)?	Nyūin shi-nakucha ikenai-no? 入院しなくちゃいけないの？
Is there anything I can do for you?	Nani-ka atashi-ni dekiru-koto aru? ♀ 何かあたしにできる事ある？ Nani-ka boku-ni dekiru-koto aru? ♂ 何か僕にできる事ある？
I just can't do it.	Kon'na-koto dekinai. こんな事できない。

I should get a better paying job.
Motto kyūryō-no ii shi-goto-o sagasa-nakucha.

Do you think you're ready to get married?
Kekkon suru kokoro-no jumbi-wa dekiteru?

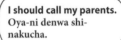

Are you trying to propose to me?
Puropōzu shiyō-to shiteru-no?

I should call my parents.
Oya-ni denwa shi-nakucha.

I have already told my parents.
Mō oya-ni itta.

My mom was ecstatic.
Haha-oya-wa ōyorokobi datta.

Dad might need some convincing.
Otōsan-wa settoku-ga hitsuyō-kamo.

You should probably hide your tattoo.
Tatū-wa kakushita-hō-ga ii-ne.

I want to meet your parents.
Goryōshin-ni atte mitai.

I want to have a small, intimate wedding.
Atto-hōmu na-kekkon-shiki-ga ii.

8

Love and Marriage

When do you want to get married?	Itsu-goro kekkon shitai? いつごろ結婚したい？
At what age do you want to marry?	Nansai-de kekkon shitai? 何歳で結婚したい？
Are you going to work after you're married?	Kekkon shite-mo hatarakitai? 結婚しても働きたい？
Do you think you're ready to get married?	Kekkon suru kokoro-no jumbi-wa dekiteru? 結婚する心の準備はできてる？

These four are "beating around the bush" questions to check if it's OK to ask the big question.

Why all these questions about marriage?	Nan-de kekkon-no-koto bakkari iu-no? 何で結婚の事ばっかり言うの？

Stop beating around the bush!	Gocha-gocha iwanai-de! ごちゃごちゃ言わないで！
Are you trying to propose to me?	Puropōzu shiyō-to shiteru-no? プロポーズしようとしてるの？
What's the question?	Nani-ga iitai-no? 何が言いたいの？
What's the answer?	Kotae-wa? 答えは？
What's on your mind?	Nani kangaeteru-no? 何考えてるの？
Will you marry me?	Kekkon shite-kureru? 結婚してくれる？

If you don't want to say this, the following four phrases are substitutes, ranked subtle to direct.

Will you make miso soup for me?	Boku-no tame-ni misoshiru-o tsukutte-kureru? ♂ 僕のためにみそ汁を作ってくれる？

Miso soup is made with soybean paste. It can be eaten at any meal, but is an important item in a traditional Japanese breakfast...

Will you use my last name?	Boku-no myōji-ni natte-kureru? ♂ 僕の名字になってくれる？

Shall we share the rest of our lives together?

Kore kara-mo zutto issho-ni ite-kurenai?
これからもずっと一緒にいてくれない?

Will you have my baby?

Boku-no kodomo-o unde-kurenai? ♂
僕の子供を産んでくれない?

I can't marry you.

Anata-to-wa kekkon-dekinai. ♀
あなたとは結婚できない。

Kimi-towa kekkon-dekinai. ♂
君とは結婚できない。

I don't want to marry you.

Anata-to-wa kekkon-shitaku-nai. ♀
あなたとは結婚したくない。

Kimi-to-wa kekkon-shitaku-nai. ♂
君とは結婚したくない。

I can't get married now.

Ima-wa kekkon-dekinai.
今は結婚できない。

Why not?

Nan-de-na-no?
何でなの?

Nande (dame-na-no)?
何で(だめなの)?

Let's get married.

Kekkon shiyō.
結婚しよう。

What are you going to do about your job/school?	Shigoto/Gakkō-o dō-suru tsumori? 仕事／学校をどうするつもり？
Are you going to quit work/school?	Shigoto/Gakkō-o yameru tsumori? 仕事／学校を辞めるつもり？
I should get a better paying job.	Motto kyūryō-no ii shi-goto-o sagasa-nakucha. もっと給料のいい仕事を探さなくちゃ。
I'd better get a second job.	Arubaito-o shita-hō-ga ii-ne. アルバイトをした方がいいね。 Arubaito-o shita-hō-ga ii-na. ♂ アルバイトをした方がいいな。

This literally means "I'd better do some part-time work," and if you're not working, this is what it means—but if you're already doing one job, it means you're thinking of getting another one.

I don't want my wife to work.	Boku-no okusan-ni-wa hataraite hoshiku-nai. ♂ 僕の奥さんには働いて欲しくない。
I'm sure the neighbors will talk about us.	Kinjo-no-hito-tachi atashi-tachi-no-koto hanasu-deshō-ne. ♀ 近所の人たちあたしたちの事話すでしょうね。

Kinjo-no-hito-tachi
boku-tachi-no-koto hanasu-
darō-ne. ♂
近所の人たち僕たちの事話す
だろうね。

Are you worried about what your neighbors might say?

Kinjo-no-hito-ga nante
iu-ka ki-ni-naru?
近所の人が何て言うか気にな
る?

Does your family care what the neighbors say?

Kinjo-no-hito-ga iu-koto
anata-no kazoku ki-ni
suru? ♀
近所の人が言う事あなたの家
族気にする?

Kinjo-no-hito-ga iu-koto
kimi-no kazoku ki-ni suru? ♂
近所の人が言う事君の家族気
にする?

Are you going to support your parents in their old age?

Ryōshin-no rōgo-no
mendō miru-no?
両親の老後の面倒見るの?

I should tell my parents.

Oya-ni itta-hō-ga ii.
親に言った方がいい。

I should call my parents.

Oya-ni denwa shi-nakucha.
親に電話しなくちゃ。

What will your parents think?

Goryōshin nan-te
omou-kana?
ご両親なんて思うかな?

ご両親 is a politer way to say "your parents" than **oya**, which you can use to refer to your own parents. Once you get married, it's common in Japan to call your spouse's parents "Mom" and "Dad," or 義母 **gibo** and 義父 **gifu**. The pronunciation is the same as when talking about your own parents, but the kanji is different.

I have already told my parents.	Mō oya-ni itta. もう親に言った。
What did they say?	Nan-te itte-ta? 何て言ってた？
Were they mad?	Okotte-ta? 怒ってた？
They must have been really surprised.	Bikkuri shite-ta deshō. びっくりしてたでしょう。
My mom was ecstatic.	Haha-oya-wa ōyorokobi datta. 母親は大喜びだった。
My dad is worried.	Chichi-oya-wa shimpai shiteru. 父親は心配してる。
They will come around soon.	Sugu-ni wakatte-kureru-yo. すぐに分かってくれるよ。
I knew they wouldn't accept it immediately.	Sō sugu-ni-wa nattoku shite-kurenai-to-wa omotteita. そうすぐには納得してくれないとは思っていた。

It might take some time.

Jikan-wa kakaru-kamo shirenai-ne.
時間はかかるかもしれないね。

Are your parents on our side?

Anata-no oya atashi-tachi-no-koto wakatte-kureta? ♀
あなたの親あたしたちの事分かってくれた?

Kimi-no oya boku-tachi-no-koto wakatte-kureta? ♂
君の親僕たちの事分かってくれた?

Will your parents help us?

Goryōshin tasukete kureru-kana? ♀/♂
ご両親助けてくれるかな?

We can live with my parents for a while.

Atashi-no oya-to shibaraku issho-ni sumeru-wa. ♀
あたしの親としばらく一緒に住めるわ。

Boku-no oya-to shibaraku issho-ni sumeru-yo. ♂
僕の親としばらく一緒に住めるよ。

How long is "a while"?

'Shibaraku'-tte dono-gurai?
「しばらく」ってどのぐらい?

I should talk to your parents (about it).

Anata-no oya-ni hanasa-nakucha. ♀
あなたの親に話さなくちゃ。

	Kimi-no oya-ni hanasa-nakucha. ♂ 君の親に話さなくちゃ。
Let me meet your parents.	Anata-no oya-ni awasete. ♀ あなたの親に会わせて。
	Kimi-no oya-ni awasete. ♂ 君の親に会わせて。
Introduce me to your family.	Anata-no kazoku-ni shōkai shite. ♀ あなたの家族に紹介して。
	Kimi-no kazoku-ni shōkai shite. ♂ 君の家族に紹介して。
I want to meet your parents.	Goryōshi-ni atte mitai. ♀/♂ ご両親に会ってみたい。
When is a good time to meet them?	Itsu-dattara tsugō-ga ii-kana? ♀/♂ いつだったら都合がいいかな?
I want to meet your parents as soon as possible.	Dekiru-dake hayaku goryōshin-ni goaisatsu shitai. 出来るだけ早くご両親にご挨拶したい。
Now is as good a time as any.	Kyō-demo ii-yo. 今日でもいいよ.
Now is not a good time.	Ima-wa yoku-nai. 今はよくない。

Maybe I shouldn't meet your parents now.

Tabun ima oya-ni awanai-hō-ga ii.
多分今親に会わない方がいい。

How about next weekend?

Raishūmatsu-wa dō?
来週末はどう？

That might work.

Ii'n-janai?
良いんじゃない？

Maybe some other time.

Chigau hi-no-hō-ga ii-to omou.
違う日のほうが良いと思う。

We can do it later.

Mata kondo-ne.
また今度ね。

Do you think your parents will accept our baby/marriage?

Goryōshin watashi-tachi/boku-tachi-no akachan/kekkon mitomete-kureru-kana? ♀/♂
ご両親私たち／僕たちの赤ちゃん／結婚認めてくれるかな？

The acceptance of cross-cultural marriages (**kokusai kekkon** 国際結婚) is growing amongst progressive-thinking Japanese. But there are still hardened attitudes against them out there, and some parents are more "protective" of their eldest son or daughter, whom they expect to be there for them when they get old. They might be scared that a foreigner would whisk their eldest away!

Tell me what to do in front of your family.	Anata-no kazoku-ni atta-toki dō-shitara ii-ka oshiete. ♀ あなたの家族に会った時どうしたらいいか教えて。 Kimi-no kazoku-ni atta-toki dō-shitara ii-ka oshiete. ♂ 君の家族に会った時どうしたらいいか教えて。

You probably shouldn't kiss or hug in front of a girl's family until they know you really well. It's OK to hold hands though.

What should I talk about?	Nani-o hanaseba ii? 何を話せばいい?
What shall I bring?	Nani motte itta-ra ii-kana? 何持って行ったら良いかな?
Tell me what to say.	Nante ittara ii-ka oshiete. 何て言ったらいいか教えて。
Do you think your family will like me?	Anata-no kazoku atashi-no-koto ki-ni-itte-kureru-kanā? ♀ あなたの家族あたしの事気に入ってくれるかなあ? Kimi-no kazoku boku-no-koto ki-ni-itte-kureru-kanā? ♂ 君の家族僕の事気に入ってくれるかなあ?

Does your mother like sweets?	Okāsan amaimono suki? お母<small>かあ</small>さん甘<small>あま</small>いもの好<small>す</small>き？

The answer is probably yes!

Should I wear a suit?	Sūtsu toka kita-hō-ga ii-no-kana? スーツとか着<small>き</small>たほうが良<small>い</small>いのかな？
You should probably hide your tattoo.	Tatū-wa kakushita-hō-ga ii-ne. タトゥーは隠<small>かく</small>したほうがいいね。
Make sure not to be late.	Chikoku shinaidene. 遅刻<small>ちこく</small>しないでね。
Does your father smoke?	Otōsan tabako su'u? お父<small>とう</small>さんタバコ吸<small>す</small>う？
Does your father drink?	Otōsan osake nomu? お父<small>とう</small>さんお酒<small>さけ</small>飲<small>の</small>む？
What's your father's hobby/work?	Otōsan-no shumi/shigoto-wa nani? お父<small>とう</small>さんの趣味<small>しゅみ</small>／仕事<small>しごと</small>は何<small>なに</small>？

Typical jobs are **kaishain** 会社員<small>かいしゃいん</small> company worker; **sararī-man** サラリーマン office worker; **ginkōin** 銀行員<small>ぎんこういん</small> banker. The answer will probably be something like one of the first two (vague) replies. After that, it's (usually!) OK to ask what company he works for **Doko-no kaisha-de hataraite-mas-ka?** どこの会社<small>かいしゃ</small>で働<small>はたら</small>いてますか？ (to his face), but don't push regarding his position.

What's your mother's hobby/work?	Okāsan-no shumi/shigoto-wa nani? お母さんの趣味／仕事は何？

Japan is still a very sexist society, and women's work is usually lower-ranking than men's. Typical jobs include OL office lady; **shufu** 主婦 housewife and **arubaito** アルバイト part-time work. If the answer is **atashi OL desu** (I'm an OL–office lady), it's probably OK to ask what company she works for **Doko-no kaisha-de hataraite-mas-ka?** どこの会社で働いてますか？ (to her face), but certainly don't ask for more information if she says **arubaito shitemasu.** アルバイトしてます。 (I work part-time)—she may be embarrassed and prefer not to say.

Who might oppose our marriage?	Dare-ga watashi-tachi-no kekkon-ni hantai suru-kana? 誰が私たちの結婚に反対するかな？ Dare-ga boku-tachi-no kekkon-ni hantai suru-kana? 誰か僕たちの結婚に反対するかな？
Who will support our marriage?	Dare-ga watashi-tachi-no kekkon-o ōen shite-kureru-kana? 誰が私たちの結婚を応援してくれるかな？ Dare-ga boku-tachi-no kekkon-o ōen shite-kureru-kana?

誰か僕たちの結婚を応援して
くれるかな?

**I think Grandma will
understand us.**

Obāchan nara wakatte-
kureru-to omou.
おばあちゃんなら分かってく
れると思う。

**Dad might need
some convincing.**

Otōsan-wa settoku-ga
hitsuyō-kamo.
お父さんは説得が必要かも。

**My mom will be
overjoyed.**

Okāsan-wa naite
yorokobu-yo.
お母さんは泣いて喜ぶよ。

When you're meeting your other half's parents for the first
time, politeness is the key—the first impression is vital!
Here are some ideas for things to say...

**How should I address
you?**

Nan-te oyobi-shitara
ii-deshō-ka?
何てお呼びしたらいいでしょ
うか?

This is no laughing matter—in Japan, children generally
call their parents and in-laws **otōsan** and **okāsan**—but
preferences vary. Getting this wrong is a very quick way to
put noses out of joint! If they prefer **otōsan** and **okāsan**, you
can then use third-person polite phrases like **Okāsan-no
shumi-wa nan des-ka?** to their faces.

Where are you from?

(Otōsan/Okāsan-wa)
Dochira-no goshusshin
des-ka?

(お父さん／お母さんは)どちらのご出身ですか?

This is a more formal and suitable question than **Dokkara kita-no?**, and unless they know you know a lot about Japan, the answer will probably not be too specific, e.g. "**Kyōto shusshin desu.** 京都出身です。I'm from Kyoto."; "**Umare-wa Kyōto des-ga, Tōkyō sodachi desu.** 生まれは京都ですが、東京育ちです。I was born in Kyoto, but I grew up in Tokyo."

What's that area known for?	**Sono chi'iki-wa nani-ga meibutsu/yūmei des-ka?** その地域は何が名物／有名ですか?
Aaah yes, I've been there.	**Aa, sō-des-ka. Watashi, itta-koto-ga arimasu.** ♀ ああ、そうですか。わたし、行ったことがあります。 **Aa, sō des-ka. Boku, itta-koto-ga arimasu.** ♂ ああ、そうですか。僕、行ったことがあります。
Have you ever been to...?	**...-e itta-koto-ga arimas-ka?** ...へ行ったことがありますか?
It's a very interesting/ busy/pretty/green city/ country, isn't it?	**Totemo omoshiroi/ nigiyaka-na/kirei-na/ shizen-ga aru machi/ tokoro des-ne.** とても面白い／にぎやかな／

きれいな／自然がある街／ところですね。

I played tennis while I was a student.

Gakusei-no-koro-wa tenisu-o yatte-imashita/ tenisubu deshita/tenisu sākuru deshita.

学生のころはテニスをやっていました／テニス部でした／テニスサークルでした。

"Tenisu-bu" is in junior or high school, "**tenisu sākuru**" is in college.

Sākuru サークル are official, sometime unofficial, clubs at universities that are based on one set sport, hobby, or activity—everything from American football to anime studies to mountaineering. In April when the school year starts, freshmen are recruited aggressively by these サークル to join. There is often heavy drinking associated with most of these gatherings.

I was in the local tennis club.

Komyunitī-no tenisu kurabu-ni haitte-imashita.

コミュニティーのテニスクラブに入っていました。

I heard that you also like tennis, Dad.

Otōsan-mo tenisu-ga osuki-to ukagai-mashita.

お父さんもテニスがお好きと伺いました。

Mom, I understand you still enjoy hiking?

Okāsan-wa ima-demo tozan-ga osuki-nan-des-yo-ne?

お母さんは今でも登山がお好
きなんですよね?

I was never a studious student, but I have always been athletic.	Boku-wa benkyō-wa nigate deshita-kedo, undō-dake-wa tokui-deshita. ♂ 僕は勉強は苦手でしたけど、運動だけは得意でした。
What did you study in college/graduate school?	Daigaku/daigakuin-dewa nani-o benkyō shite-rasshattan-des-ka? 大学／大学院では何を勉強してらっしゃったんですか?

HONORIFIC LANGUAGE: KEIGO 敬語

It's very important when speaking to older Japanese people, especially your significant other's parents at an early stage in the relationship, to use very formal (**sonkeigo** 尊敬語) speech.

Instead of saying **shite-ita-no des-ka?** していたのですか? to mean "were you...ing?" you should say **shite-rashita-no des-ka?** してらしたのですか?, which is even politer.

OTHER EXAMPLES:

"Thank you for coming over" 来てくれてありがとう (casual)
Kite-kurute arigatō → わざわざお越し頂いてありがとうございます。 **Waza-waza okoshi-itadaite arigatō gozaimasu.**

If you can say this smoothly the first time you meet your sweetheart's parents, you're golden!

I heard　　　　　　kiki-mashita 聞きました

→ ukagai-mashita 伺いました

Would you like to see?　mimasu? 見ます？

→ goran-ni nari-masu?
ご欄になります？

please eat　　　　　tabete-kudasai 食べて下さい

→ meshiagatte-kudasai
召し上がって下さい

I will eat (what you　tabemasu 食べます
gave me)

→ itadakimasu いただきます
[better to use this word]

How much will the　　Kekkon-shiki-no hiyō
wedding cost?　　　ikura gurai kakaru-no?
結婚式の費用いくらぐらいか
かるの？

We have to hurry to　Isoide kekkon-shiki-o
have the wedding.　age-nakucha.
急いで結婚式をあげなくちゃ。

We should begin　　Ima-kara yōi shita-hō-ga ii.
preparing now.　　今から用意した方がいい。

Should we have a　　Seiyō-shiki-to Nihon-
Japanese or a Western-　shiki, dotchi-ni suru?
style wedding?　　西洋式と日本式、どっちにす
る？

I'm okay with either option.

Dochira-demo ii des-yo.
どちらでもいいですよ。

I'll go along with whatever she wants to do.

Kanojo-no suki-na-hō-de boku-wa ii des-yo. ♂
彼女の好きな方で僕はいいですよ。

Do you want to have a big or small wedding?

Kekkon-shiki-wa hade-na-hō-ga ii? Jimi-na-hō-ga ii?
結婚式は派手な方がいい?地味な方がいい?

How many people will we invite?

Nan-nin gurai shōtai suru?
何人ぐらい招待する?

Where should we have the wedding?

Shiki-wa doko de ageru?
式はどこで挙げる?

I want to have a destination wedding.

Rizōto wedingu-ga ii-na.
リゾートウェディングがいいな。

I want to invite all of my relatives.

Shinseki-mo min'na yobitai.
親戚もみんな呼びたい。

I want to have a small, intimate wedding.

Atto hōmu-na kekkon-shiki-ga ii.
アットホームな結婚式がいい。

I just want to invite our immediate family.

Kazoku dake-de agetai.
家族だけで挙げたい。

I have no idea!

Zenzen wakan'nai!
全然わかんない!

Weddings in Japan cost a small fortune, going from about 1,000,000 yen and above, to include everything. Luckily, there is a tradition in Japan called ご祝儀 (**goshūgi**), which literally means "celebratory money," which is given to the newlywed couple at their wedding, instead of a wedding gift. Usually each guest gives about 20,000 to 30,000 yen wrapped in a fancy envelope. Most couples plan and execute their weddings with an expectation of receiving a certain amount of money from their guests, which makes the actual out-of-pocket expense significantly smaller. Weddings are changing with the times, with many couples going for **suma-kon** スマ婚 (meaning "smart wedding"). This lets the couple pay half of the wedding expenses upfront, and pay the rest after receiving money from their guests. The wedding can also be a **rizo-kon** リゾ婚 ("resort wedding") where only family members and maybe a few close friends are invited. Another option is to have a **resutoran wedingu** レストランウェディング ("restaurant wedding"), which is also smaller and more intimate. If you and your fiance want to go the traditional route, there are numerous books in Japanese outlining the traditions and customs of Japanese style, or Western-Japanese style weddings. This includes seating arrangements, how to greet guests, and give appropriate speeches.

9

Health

You have a nice figure. Sutairu ii-ne. ♀
スタイルいいね。
Sutairu ii-na. ♂
スタイルいいな。

Sutairu ga ii-ne is only used when speaking to women.

You're slim. Yaseteru-ne.
やせてるね。
Yaseteru-na. ♂
やせてるな。
Surimu-dane.
スリムだね。
Surimu-dana. ♂
スリムだな。

You have huge muscles! Kin'niku sugoi-ne.
筋肉すごいね。

You're skinny. Hosoi-ne.
細いね。

Have I gained weight?	Futotta-to omou? 太ったと思う？
Did you lose weight?	Yaseta? やせた？
Did you gain weight?	Chotto futotta-kanā? ちょっと太ったかなあ？ Futotta? 太った？
Have you put on a few pounds?	Chotto futotta? ちょっと太った？

As in the West, if you're going to ask this (of a girl especially), it's better to couch it softly!

Do you think I need to diet?	Daietto shita-hō-ga ii-to omou? ダイエットした方がいいと思う？
Maybe you could try dieting?	Daietto shite mitara? ダイエットしてみたら？
I think you look healthy.	Kenkō-teki-ni mieru-kedo. 健康的に見えるけど。
Has a good built.	Taikaku-ga ii. 体格が良い。

This is a nice way to say someone is overweight and can be used to refer to both men and women.

Skinny-buff	Hoso-matcho 細マッチョ

A lot of Japanese men are **hoso-matcho** without trying, just because some of them have very little body fat which accentuates their average level muscle mass.*

No, I like the way you are now.	Uun, sono-mama-de ii-yo. ううん、そのままでいいよ。
You need to go on a diet.	Daietto shita-hō-ga ii-yo. ダイエットした方がいいよ。
I'm on a diet now.	Ima daietto shiteru. 今ダイエットしてる。
I'm a vegetarian.	Atashi bejitarian. ♀ あたしベジタリアン。 Boku bejitarian. ♂ 僕ベジタリアン。
I don't eat fried food.	Agemono-wa tabenai. 揚げ物は食べない。
I try not to eat sweet food (as much as I can).	Dekirudake amaimono tabenai-yō-ni shiteru. できるだけ甘いもの食べないようにしてる。
I don't have time to cook proper meals.	Chanto shita ryōri-o tsukuru jikan-ga nai. ちゃんとした料理を作る時間がない。
We could try cooking together.	Issho-ni ryōri shite-miru? 一緒に料理してみる？

I know some healthy restaurants.

Herushī-na resutoran-o shitteru.
ヘルシーなレストランを知ってる。

You should eat less snacks.

Oyatsu-o tabenai-hō-ga ii-yo.
おやつを食べない方がいいよ。

You shouldn't drink so much beer.

Bīru-o son'na-ni nomanai-hō-ga ii-yo.
ビールをそんなに飲まない方がいいよ。

You should stop smoking.

Tabako yameta-hō-ga ii-yo.
タバコ止めた方がいいよ。

Stop smoking.

Tabako yamete.
タバコ止めて。

Tabako yamena-yo.
タバコ止めなよ。

Do you exercise?

Undō suru?
運動する？

I'm too lazy.

Mendokusai.
めんどくさい。

We can do it together.

Issho-ni shiyō-yo.
一緒にしようよ。

Let's play basketball together next weekend.	Rai-shūmatsu basuke yarōyo. 来週末バスケやろうよ。
I suck at sports.	Undō-onchi nano/nanda. ♀/♂ 運動音痴なの／なんだ。
What type of exercise do you do?	Don'na undō suru-no? どんな運動するの？
I run three kilometers every day.	Mainichi san-kiro hashiru. 毎日3キロ走る。
I go to the gym.	Jimu-ni iku. ジムに行く。
I go to the pool.	Pūru-ni iku. プールに行く。
I like to swim.	Oyogu-no-ga suki. 泳ぐのが好き。

After a good exercise session, say **Koshi-ga itai** 腰が痛い, which means "My back hurts." People listening to you will really think you had sex the night before and that is the reason for your backache.

I play soccer/ tennis/golf.	Sakkā/tenisu/gorufu-o yaru. サッカー／テニス／ゴルフを やる。

10

Curses and Insults

The following curses are commonly uttered:

Weak

I can't believe you.	Shinji-rarenai. 信じられない。
Cut it out.	Yamete-yo. やめてよ。

Average

Idiot!	Baka! ばか!
You	Anta. ♀ あんた。

Strong

Imbecile!	Baka-yarō! バカ野郎!

Go to hell/die!	**Shine!** 死ね！
I fucking hate you.	**Dai-kirai** 大嫌い。
You	**Omē./Temē.** おめえ。／てめえ。
What a coincidence (seeing you here).	**Kon'na tokoro-de au-towa-ne** こんな所で会うとはね。
Fancy seeing you in a place like this.	**Kon'na tokoro-de au-nante.** こんな所で会うなんて。

These can be used with the same sarcastic intent as in English.

This is a pain (bother).	**Mendōkusai.** 面倒臭い。

This common phrase is usually shortened to **mendokusai** めんどくさい.

Who do you think you are?	**Nani-sama?** 何様？
Whore/slut.	**Kōshū benjo.** 公衆便所

This implies that she'll let anyone "use" her.

She's stupid!   **Aitsu baka-dayo!** ♂
あいつばかだよ！

Baka is one word that varies hugely in strength between regions. In Kantō, it's a moderate insult; in Kansai, it's about as harsh as it gets—there, **aho** あほ has a similar strength to **baka** in Kantō.

Wrong!   **Chigau-yo!**
違うよ！

That's not right!   **Chigau-mon!** ♀
違うもん！

                               Chigau-wa-yo! ♀
違うわよ！

                               Chigau-yo!
違うよ！

Shut up!   **Damatte-yo!/Damare-yo!** ♀
黙ってよ！／黙れよ！

Who do you think   **Erasō-ni iuna-yo!** ♂
you are?   偉そうに言うなよ！

You're dirty!   **Kitanai!**
(Your relationship is   汚い！
shameful.)

Don't be jealous!   **Yakimochi yakuna-yo!** ♂
やきもちやくなよ！

This is a good response to any of the above phrases.

Grow up!   **Gaki!**
ガキ！

**Don't act like a child/
don't be childish!**

Kodomo mitai-na-koto
shinaide! (weak)
子供見たいなことしないで!

Gaki janēn-dakara!
(stronger)
ガキじゃねえんだから!

Act your age.

Ittai ikutsu-dayo.
いったいいくつだよ。

This literally means "How old are you?" 君は何歳／いくつ?

**Don't get too big for
your boots.**

Jū-nen hayai.
十年早い。

十年早い is a phrase heard in movies and dramas, but not
used so much in real life.

Don't make me laugh.

Warawase-nai-de. ♀
笑わせないで。

Warawase-runa-yo. ♂
笑わせるなよ。

**Stop acting stupid!/
Don't joke around
with me!**

Fuzake-nai-deyo! ♀
ふざけないでよ!

Fuzake-runa-yo! ♂
ふざけるなよ!

Fuzaken-janē-yo! ♂
ふざけんじゃねえよ!*

*This is used especially when someone is being cheeky or
has underestimated the speaker's power or status.

You're crazy!

Atama okashiin-janai-no?
頭おかしいんじゃないの?

That's stupid!	**Baka-mitai!** ばかみたい！ **Baka-jan!** ばかじゃん！

じゃん is both regional and now a bit out-dated. It is/was used in the Yokohama area. These days, **jane?** 〜じゃね? is a lot more common, which is close in meaning and usage to "..., isn't it?" Although it is a phrase used more often by men, women often use it in the company of fellow females.

What you did was stupid!	**Baka-da!** ばかだ！
You're stupid!/ **You're an idiot!**	**Baka!** ばか！ **Baka-yarō!** ♂ ばかやろう！
Don't act stupid!/ **Stop acting stupid!**	**Baka yamete-yo!** ♀ ばか止めてよ！ **Baka yamero-yo!** ♂ ばか止めろよ！ **Baka yamena-yo!** ♀ ばか止めなよ！ **Baka yatten-janē-yo!** ♂ ばかやってんじゃねえよ！
What are you doing?	**Nani shiten-no?/Nani yatten-no?** 何してんの？／何やってんの？

What the hell are you doing?

Nani yattenda-yo!
何やってんだよ！

You shouldn't have done that.

Ah-ah, nani yatten-daka.
あーあ、何やってんだか。

Sore shinakya yokatta-noni.
それしなきゃよかったのに。

How dare you!

Nan-de son'na-koto dekiru-no! ♀
何でそんな事できるの？

Nan-de son'na-koto dekirun-da! ♂
何でそんな事できるんだ？

Don't you have something to do? (Stop bothering me!)

Hoka-ni suru-koto nai-no?
他にする事ないの？

You ain't got the balls!

Tama tsuiten-no?
玉ついてんの？

Means you're lacking in courage.

Chinchin chiisai! ♂
ちんちん小さい！

This literally means "You have a small penis!" As you'd expect, it's a very serious insult!

You haven't changed a bit.

Zenzen kawatte-nai-ne.
全然変わってないね。

You really piss me off.

Maji-de mukatsuku.
マジでムカつく。

I've got guts!	**Konjō-wa aru-sa!** 根性はあるさ！
Don't make me mad.	**Okorase-nai-de(-yo).** ♀ 怒らせないで(よ)。
	Okoraseru-na. ♂ 怒らせるな。
I'm going mad/ Fuck this! (broad meaning)	**Mukatsuita!** むかついた！
	Mukatsuku! むかつく！
Fuck you!/Go to hell!	**Kutabare!** ♂ くたばれ！
	Shine! ♂ 死ね！
Get out of here!/ Fuck off!	**Kiero!** ♂ きえろ！
	Mukō itte-yo! ♀ 向こうに行ってよ！
	Atchi itte-yo! ♀ あっち行ってよ！
	Atchi ike-yo! ♂ あっち行けよ！
	Dokka itchimae-yo! ♂ どっか行っちまえよ！
I'm leaving!	**Mō iku!** もう行く！
	Mō iku-yo! ♂ もう行くよ！

I don't (even) want to think about it.
Kangae-taku(-mo) nai.

What does that mean?
Dōiu imi?

Let's not get serious now.
Ima majime-na hanashi-wa shitakunai.

We've known each other for three months now.
Atashi-tachi shiriatte-kara sankagetsu-ni naru-no(ne).

I want to know what you're feeling.
Anata-ga dō omotteru-ka shiritai.

I'll do anything to make you forgive me.
Yurushite-kureru-nara nan-demo suru-yo.

Please understand how I feel.
Atashi-no kimochi-mo kangaete.

Anything?
Nan-demo?

I don't play around.
Boku-wa asondenai-yo.

Don't be upset.
Okoruna-yo.

I promise.
Yakusoku suru.

Promise it will never happen again.
Mō zettai shinaitte yakusoku shite.

11

Lovers' Arguments

It wasn't your day, was it?

Kyō-wa tsuite-nakatta-nē?
今日はついてなかったねえ。

It's boring, isn't it?

Tsuman'nai-nē?
つまんないねえ。

Do you feel comfortable in public with me?

Atashi-to issho-ni dearuku-no ki-ni-naru? ♀
あたしと一緒に出歩くの気になる?

Boku-to issho-ni dearuku-no ki-ni-naru? ♂
僕と一緒に出歩くの気になる?

I don't want you to get hurt on my account.

Atashi-no sei-de iya-na omoi sase-taku-nai. ♀
あたしのせいでいやな思いさせたくない。

Boku-no sei-de iya-na
omoi sase-taku-nai. ♂
僕のせいでいやな思いさせた
くない。

**Do you care what they
think?**

Min'na-ga dō omou-ka
ki-ni-naru?
皆がどう思うか気になる?

**Don't let it bother you
(what others think).**

Hoka-no-hito-no-koto
ki-ni shinaide. ♀
他の人のこと気にしないで。

Hoka-no-hito-no-koto
ki-ni-suru-na-yo. ♂
他の人のこと気にするなよ。

Don't be upset.

Okoranaide-yo. ♀
怒らないでよ。

Okoruna-yo. ♂
怒るなよ。

**Does your family know
about us?**

Anata-no kazoku
atashi-tachi-no-koto
shitteru? ♀
あなたの家族あたしたちのこ
と知ってる?

Kimi-no kazoku boku-
tachi-no-koto shitteru? ♂
君の家族僕たちのこと知って
る?

I told my family about you.

Kazoku-ni anata-no-koto hanashita. ♀
家族にあなたのこと話した。

Kazoku-ni kimi-no-koto hanashita. ♂
家族に君のこと話した。

Do you think we should see each other again?

Atashi-tachi mata attara ii-to omou? ♀
あたしたちまた会ったらいいと思う?

Boku-tachi mata attara ii-to omou? ♂
僕たちまた会ったらいいと思う?

Tell me, what do you think?

Dō omou? Oshiete.
どう思う? 教えて。

Be honest.

Shōjiki-ni hanashite.
正直に話して。

You don't understand.

Anata/kimi-ni-wa wakaranai. ♀/♂
あなた/君にはわからない。

I need some space.

Chotto sotto shite-oite.
ちょっとそっとしておいて。

Talk to me.

Nani kangaeteru-ka oshiete.
何考えてるか教えて。

| Let's not talk about this right now. | Ima hanashi-taku-nai.
今話したくない。 |

| Please don't go. | Ikanai-de.
行かないで。 |

| Do you think we should see each other again? | Watashi-tachi mata atte-mo iito omou?
私たちまた会ってもいいと思う？ |

| You don't know. | Anata-wa shiranai-to omou. ♀
あなたは知らないと思う。
Kimi-wa shiranai-to omou. ♂
君は知らないと思う。 |

| We've known each other for three months now. | Atashi-tachi shiriatte-kara sankagetsu-ni naru-no(ne). ♀
あたしたち知り合ってから3か月になるの（ね）。
Boku-tachi shiriatte-kara sanka-getsu-ni naru-nā/ne. ♂
僕たち知り合ってから3か月になるなあ／ね。 |

When saying this to someone else, say... **ni naru-nā**. To your partner, a final **ne** with a (slight) rising intonation is better.

| We can make it work. | Dō ni-ka naru-yo.
どうにかなるよ。 |

I want to know what you're feeling.	**Anata-ga dō omotteru-ka shiritai.** ♀ あなたがどう思ってるか知りたい。 **Kimi-ga dō omotteru-ka shiritai.** ♂ 君がどう思ってるか知りたい。
It'll all change.	**Subete kawaru-yo.** 全て変わるよ。
Let's not get serious now.	**Ima majime-na hanashi-wa shitaku-nai.** 今真面目な話はしたくない。

The use of "let's" here is very Japanese, as it invites the other party into the decision-making process, a part of the typical Japanese subtlety. Directly stating one's wishes will halve the normal runaround, but will put off those who prefer indirectness.

I don't want to get serious.	**Maji-ni nari-taku-nai.** マジになりたくない。
I don't (even) want to think about it.	**Kangae-taku(-mo) nai.** 考えたく(も)ない。

This is a very strong phrase—use it with care!

What does that mean?	**Dō-iu imi?** どういう意味？
Don't cry.	**Nakanai-de/nakuna-yo.** ♀/♂ 泣かないで／泣くなよ。

Don't be sad.　　　　　Kanashima-naide.
　　　　　　　　　　　　悲しまないで。

Cheer up.　　　　　　　Genki dashite.
　　　　　　　　　　　　元気出して。

Don't worry; be happy.　Shimpai-shinaide, genki
　　　　　　　　　　　　dashite.
　　　　　　　　　　　　心配しないで、元気出して。

Let's talk about　　　　Mata kondo hanasō.
this later.　　　　　　　また今度話そう。

Let's change the　　　　Chotto hanashi-ga kawaru
subject.　　　　　　　　kedo...
　　　　　　　　　　　　ちょっと話が変わるけど...。
　　　　　　　　　　　　Hanashi-o kaeyō.
　　　　　　　　　　　　話を変えよう。

By the way,...　　　　　Tokoro-de,...
　　　　　　　　　　　　ところで...

Don't change the　　　　Hanashi-o kaenai-de. ♀
subject.　　　　　　　　話を変えないで。
　　　　　　　　　　　　Hanashi-o kaeru-na. ♂
　　　　　　　　　　　　話を変えるな。

Please listen to me/　　(Tanomu-kara/
let me explain.　　　　　Onegai-dakara) hanashi-o
　　　　　　　　　　　　kiite.
　　　　　　　　　　　　(頼むから／お願いだから)話
　　　　　　　　　　　　を聞いて。

Men usually say **tanomukara,...** whereas women usually say **onegaidakara...** when making a request.

I was only joking.	Tada-no jōdan-dayo. ただの冗談だよ。
Don't take it so seriously.	Son'na-ni maji-ni toranai-de. ♀ そんなにマジに取らないで。 Son'na-ni maji-ni toruna-yo. ♂ そんなにマジに取るなよ。
I don't play around.	Atashi-wa asonde-nai-wayo. ♀ あたしは遊んでないわよ。 Boku-wa asonde-nai-yo. ♂ 僕は遊んでないよ。
I was busy playing around.	Asobi-makutteta. 遊びまくってた。
Don't do that again.	Mō son'na-koto shinaide. もうそんな事しないで。
It's fine/I'm over it.	Sono-koto-wa mō ii-yo. そのことはもういいよ。
I'm not mad anymore.	Mō okotte-nai-wa. ♀ もう怒ってないわ。 Mō okotte-nai-yo. ♂ もう怒ってないよ。

Are you still mad?

Mada okotteru?
まだ怒ってる?

**You're still mad,
aren't you?**

Mada okotteru-deshō? ♀
まだ怒ってるでしょう?

Mada okotteru-darō? ♂
まだ怒ってるだろう?

I was wrong.

Atashi-ga machigatteta-wa. ♀
あたしが間違ってたわ。

Boku-ga machigatteta-yo. ♂
僕が間違ってたよ。

**I shouldn't have
done that.**

Shinakya yokatta.
しなきゃよかった。

Surun-ja nakatta.
するんじゃなかった。

**I don't know why I
did that.**

Nan-de sō shita-ka
wakan'nai.
何でそうしたか分かんない。

**I think I was too
excited.**

Sugoku moriagatteta.
すごく盛り上がってた。

Sugoku waku-waku shiteta.
すごくわくわくしてた。

**I think I was too
nervous.**

Chotto kinchō shiteta.
ちょっと緊張してた。

Chotto ochikondeta.
ちょっと落ち込んでた。

I was out of my mind.

Jibun-demo naze-ka
wakan'nai.
自分でもなぜか分かんない。

**It was silly of me
(to do that).**

Baka-na-koto shita-nā.
ばかな事したなあ。

**You have so much
more than they do.**

Anata-wa min'na-ni
naimono-o motteru. ♀
あなたは皆にないものを持っ
てる。

Kimi-wa min'na-ni
naimono-o motteru. ♂
君は皆にないものを持ってる。

**If you change your
mind, let me know.**

Moshi ki-ga kawatta-ra
oshiete.
もし気が変わったら教えて。

**What changed your
mind?**

Nan-de ki-ga kawatta-no?
何で気が変わったの？

**I didn't mean to
hurt you.**

Kizutsukeru tsumori-wa
nakatta.
傷つけるつもりはなかった。

**I should've thought
about it more.**

Motto kangaereba
yokatta.
もっと考えればよかった。

**I hurt your feelings,
didn't I?**

Kanji warukatta deshō? ♀
感じ悪かったでしょう？

Kanji warukatta darō? ♂
感じ悪かっただろう？

I know I hurt your feelings.

Kizutsuketa-ne. ♀
傷付けたね。

I was out of it.

Shōki-ja nakatta.
正気じゃなかった。

I wasn't myself.

Dōka shiteta.
どうかしてた。

I take it back.

Ima-no torikeshite.
今の取り消して。

You are always the one starting it.

Anata/omae ga itsumo
kenka utte-kuru-kara
(kō-narunda-yo).
あなた／おまえがいつもけん
か売ってくるから（こうなるん
んだよ）。

Used as an excuse for something that happened, blaming it on the other person.

Why are you always like this?

Nan-de ittsumo kō-nano?
なんでいっつもこうなの？

Let's make up.

Nakanaori shiyō.
仲直りしよう。

Let's try to make this work.

Gambatte miyō-yo.
頑張ってみようよ。

I'll do anything to make you forgive me.	Yurushite-kureru-nara nandemo suru-wa. ♀ 許してくれるなら何でもするわ。 Yurushite-kureru-nara nandemo suru-yo. ♂ 許してくれるなら何でもするよ。
Anything?	Nan-demo? 何でも？
I was blind to the truth.	Nani-ga hontō-ka-wakarana-katta. 何が本当か分からなかった。
Please understand how I feel.	Atashi-no kimochi-mo kangaete. ♀ あたしの気持ちも考えて。 Boku-no kimochi-mo kangaete. ♂ 僕の気持ちも考えて。
You didn't even listen to me.	Kiite-mo kure-nakatta. 聞いてもくれなかった。
Let's get back. together	Yori-o modosō. ヨリを戻そう。
Promise it will never happen again.	Mō zettai shinaitte yakusoku shite. もう絶対しないって約束して。

This should be used in context when the topic under discussion is clear to both parties.

I promise.	Yakusoku suru. 約束する。
Please take me back/ forgive me.	Yurushite. 許して。
I'm always doing silly things.	Atashitte itsumo baka-na- koto suru-yone. ♀ あたしっていつもばかな事す るよね。 Bokutte itsumo baka-na- koto suru-yona. ♂ 僕っていつもばかな事するよ な。
I feel so lonely.	Samishii. 寂しい。
I can't concentrate.	Nan-nimo shūchū dekinai. 何にも集中出来ない。
I keep thinking about you.	Anta/omae-no-koto bakari kangaeteru-yo. あなた／お前のことばかり考 えてるよ。
I'm losing sleep.	Nemure-nai-no. ♀ 眠れないの。 Nemure-nain-da. ♂ 眠れないんだ。

You were the first and you'll be the last.

Anata-ga saisho-de, saigo-yo. ♀
あなたが最初で、最後よ。

Kimi-ga saisho-de, saigo-da. ♂
君が最初で、最後だ。

Whenever you need someone, I'll always be there.

Nani-ka attara, itsu-demo itte.
何かあったら、いつでも言って。

Whatever you want I'll give it to you.

Nan-demo hoshii-mono ageru.
何でも欲しい物あげる。

Come back to me.

Atashi-no-moto-ni modotte-kite. ♀
あたしのもとに戻って来て。

Boku-no-moto-ni modotte-kite. ♂
僕のもとに戻って来て。

I believe you still love me.

Mada sukitte shinjiteru.
まだ好きって信じてる。

Don't throw away this chance.

Kono chansu-o nogasanai-de.
このチャンスを逃さないで。

It might be your last.

Saigo-kamo shirenai.
最後かもしれない。

12

Broken Intercourse

You forgot my birthday?	Watashi/boku-no tanjōbi wasureteta-no? 私／僕の誕生日忘れてたの？
You forgot our anniversary.	Kinenbi wasureteta deshō. ♀ 記念日忘れてたでしょう。 Kinenbi wasureteta darō. ♂ 記念日忘れてただろう。
Are you serious? Again?	Maji-de? Mata? マジで？また？
Why didn't you call me?	Nan-de denwa kure-nakatta-no? 何で電話くれなかったの？
I waited all night/a long time for your call.	Hitoban-jū/Zutto denwa-o matteta. 一晩中／ずっと電話を待ってた。

I was just about to call you.	Ima denwa suru-tokoro-datta. 今電話するところだった。
I tried to call you.	Denwa shita-noyo. ♀ 電話したのよ。
	Denwa shitanda-yo. ♂ 電話したんだよ。
I was busy.	Isogashi-katta. 忙しかった。
I had no change in my wallet.	Kozeni-ga nakatta. 小銭がなかった。
My (phone's) battery was flat.	Batterī-ga kireta. バッテリーが切れた。
I couldn't get any reception.	Dempa-ga warukute. 電波が悪くて。
My phone died.	Batterī-ga kireta. バッテリーが切れた。
I was out of range.	Dempa-ga yowa-katta. 電波が弱かった。
Where were you?	Doko-ni ita-no? どこにいたの？
That's a secret!	Himitsu-yo! ♀ 秘密よ！
	Himitsu-dayo! ♂ 秘密だよ！

**Don't trick me/
lie to me.**

Uso tsukanai-de. ♀
嘘つかないで。

Uso tsukuna-yo. ♂
嘘つくなよ。

You lied to me.

Usotsuita-deshō.
嘘ついたでしょう。

Usotsuita-darō. ♂
嘘ついただろう。

Stop lying to me.

Mō uso-wa yamete! ♀
もう嘘は止めて！

**I know you're lying
to me.**

Uso-datte wakatteru.
嘘だって分かってる。

Lies!

Uso bakkari!
嘘ばっかり！

Just stop.

Mō yamete.
もうやめて。

I'm so tired of this.

Mō tsukareta.
もう疲れた。

**I can't trust you
any more.**

Anata-no-koto mō
shinji-rarenai. ♀
あなたの事もう信じられない。

Kimi-no-koto mō shinji-
rarenai. ♂
君の事もう信じられない。

Everything you've said is a lie.	Anata-ga itta-koto-wa zembu uso-datta. あなたが言ったことは全部嘘だった。
Let me speak frankly.	Hontō-no-koto iwasete. 本当の事言わせて。
I'm sorry, but...	Warui-kedo,... 悪いけど...
Do you want to know the truth?	Hontō-no-koto shiritai? 本当の事知りたい？
You're so selfish!	Maji-de jikochū-dane! マジで自己中だね！
You never think about how I might feel.	Watashi/boku-no kimochi nanka ki-ni-mo kakete kurenai. 私／僕の気持ちなんか気にもかけてくれない。
I don't want to hear it.	Kiki-taku-nai. 聞きたくない。
Who am I to you?	Atashi-wa anata-no nan-nano? ♀ あたしはあなたの何なの？ Boku-wa kimi-no nan-nanda? ♂ 僕は君の何なんだ？

**Who do you think
I am?**

Atashi-o nanda-to
omotteru-no? ♀
あたしを何だと思ってるの？

Boku-o nanda-to
omotterun-da? ♂
僕を何だと思ってるんだ？

**Don't pretend nothing
happened.**

Nani-mo nakatta-yō-na
kao-shinaide. ♀
何もなかったような顔しない
で。

Nani-mo nakatta-yō-na
kao-suruna. ♂
何もなかったような顔するな。

**How can you act like
that (to me)?**

Dō-shite son'na-kao suru-
no? ♀
どうしてそんな顔するの？

Dō-shite son'na-kao surun-
da? ♂
どうしてそんな顔するんだ？

You made me do it.

Anata-ga sō saseta-no. ♀
あなたがそうさせたの。

Kimi-ga sō sasetan-darō. ♂
君がそうさせたんだろう。

Don't make excuses.

Iiwake-shinaide. ♀
言い訳しないで。

Iiwake-suru-na. ♂
言い訳するな。

What are you doing?
Dō-iu tsumori?

Don't embarrass me.
Haji kakaseru-nayo.

Who was she/he?
Ano otoko dare?

Stop playing these games.
Gomakasu-no-wa yamero-yo.

Don't act like I'm yours.
Wagamono-gao shinai-de.

Let me be me.
Atashi-ni kamawanai-deyo.

Don't think that I'm only yours.
Atashi-wa anata-dake-no mono janai-wayo.

I wish you had more experience.
Motto keiken hōfu nara ii-noni.

It was just a game, wasn't it?
Tada-no asobi-dattan-da?

I've already thrown them away!
Mō suteta(wa)-yo!

Give me back all the presents I gave to you!
Boku-ga ageta-mono zembu kaese-yo!

13

Breaking Up!

You told me you loved me.	Sukitte itta-janai/ janai-ka. ♀/♂ 好きって言ったじゃない／ じゃないか。
Are you telling me you don't love me anymore?	Atashi-no-koto mō suki janai-no? ♀ あたしの事もう好きじゃない の？ Boku-no-koto mō suki janai-no? ♂ 僕の事もう好きじゃないの？
I'm tired of you.	Anata-ni-wa akita. ♀ あなたには飽きた。 Kimi-ni-wa akita. ♂ 君には飽きた。
Are you tired of me?	Atashi-ni akita-no? ♀ あたしに飽きたの？

Boku-ni akita-no? ♂
僕に飽きたの？

I knew it wouldn't work.

Dame-datte wakatteta.
だめだって分かってた。

Dame-datte wakatteta-yo. ♂
だめだって分かってたよ。

You've changed.

Kawatta-ne.
変わったね。

You messed up my life.

Atashi-no jinsei mechakucha-ni shita. ♀
あたしの人生めちゃくちゃにした。

Boku-no jinsei mechakucha-ni shita. ♂
僕の人生めちゃくちゃにした。

Don't hurt me anymore.

Mō kizu-tsukenai-de.
もう傷つけないで。

Let's not tie each other down.

Otagai-ni kanshō suru-no-wa yame-yō.
お互いに干渉するのは止めよう。

This implies "Let's see other people."

You're the one who said "Let's stop seeing each other."

Anata-ga mō awanaitte ittan-desho. ♀
あなたがもう会わないって言ったんでしょ。

Kimi-ga mō awanaitte
ittan-darō. ♂
君がもう会わないって言った
んだろう。

**You take me for
granted.**

Atashi-o riyō shiteru-
deshō? ♀
あたしを利用してるでしょう?

Boku-o riyō shiteru-darō?
♂
僕を利用してるだろう?

This is a very strong accusation—don't use it lightly!

**I can't believe you
were just using me.**

Riyō shiteta-dake dattan-
dane.
利用してただけだったんだね。

What are you doing?

Dō-iu tsumori?
どういうつもり?

**Don't tell me what
to do.**

Urusaku-iwanai-de.
うるさく言わないで。

**I don't tell you what
to do.**

Urusaku ittenai-deshō. ♀
うるさく言ってないでしょう。

Urusaku ittenai-darō. ♂
うるさく言ってないだろう。

I'll do whatever I want.　Atashi-wa katte-ni suru-wa. ♀

あたしは勝手にするわ。

Boku-wa katte-ni suru-yo. ♂

僕は勝手にするよ。

Don't try to change me.　Watashi-o kaeyō-to

shinaide. ♀

私を変えようとしないで。

Boku-o kaeyō-to shinaide. ♂

僕を変えようとしないで。

I can't compromise　Watashi/Boku-wa kore-ijō

anymore.　dakyō dekinai. ♀/♂

私/僕はこれ以上妥協できな

い。

I can't make you　Anata/Kimi-no-koto-o

happy.　shiawase-ni dekinai. ♀/♂

あなた／君のことを幸せにでき

ない。

I can't be what you　Anata-no risō-ni-wa

want me to be.　nare-nai. ♀

あなたの理想にはなれない。

Kimi-no risō-ni-wa nare-

nai. ♂

君の理想にはなれない。

Let me be me.　Atashi-ni kamawanai-deyo.

あたしに構わないでよ。

Boku-ni kamawanai-de.

僕に構わないで。

Leave me alone.	Hottoite. ほっといて。
Stop following me around.	Tsuite-kuru-no-wa yamete. 付いて来るのは止めて。 Tsuite-konai-de. 付いて来ないで。 Tsuite-kuru-na! ♂ 付いて来るな！
There is nothing left to talk about.	Mō hanasu-koto nante-nai. もう話すことなんてない。
We are not right for each other.	Otagai-ni fusawashiku-nai-yo. お互いにふさわしくないよ。
We are destroying each other.	Otagai kizutsuke-atteru. お互い傷つけあってる。
I am not happy anymore.	Shiawase-janai. 幸せじゃない。
It's too late.	Mō osoi. もう遅い。
I need something more.	Mono-tarinai. 物足りない。
You deserve someone better.	Motto fusawashii-hito-ga iru-yo. もっとふさわしい人がいるよ。

I want us to still be friends.	Tomodachi-de itai. 友達でいたい。
I will never be able to see you as a friend.	Tomodachi-ni mirenai. 友達にみれない。
I don't want to hurt you anymore.	Koreijō kizutsuketaku nai. これ以上傷つけたくない。
Don't embarrass me.	Haji kakasenai-de. 恥かかせないで。 Haji kakaseruna-yo. ♂ 恥かかせるなよ。
Don't disappoint me (again).	(Mō) gakkari-sasenai-de. (もう)がっかりさせないで。 (Mō) gakkari-saseru-na. ♂ (もう)がっかりさせるな。
I'm disappointed in you.	Anata-ni-wa gakkari-shita. ♀ あなたにはがっかりした。 Kimi-ni-wa gakkari-shita. ♂ 君にはがっかりした。
How many girls have you made cry?	Ima-made nan-nin nakasete kita-no? ♀ 今まで何人泣かせて来たの？
How many boys have you made cry?	Ima-made nan-nin nakasete kitan-da? ♂ 今まで何人泣かせて来たんだ？

Think about the way you acted/treated me!	**Anata-ga don'na-koto shita-ka kangaete-mite-yo!** ♀ あなたがどんな事したか考えてみてよ!
	Kimi-ga don'na-koto shita-ka kangaete-miro! ♂ 君がどんな事したか考えてみろ!
Have you been fucking with me this whole time?	**Zutto asobi datta-no?** ずっと遊びだったの?
I didn't mean to.	**Son'na tsumori-ja nakatta.** そんなつもりじゃなかった。
It was just a game, wasn't it?	**Dōse asobi dattan-desho?** ♀ どうせ遊びだったんでしょ?
	Tada-no asobi-dattan-da? ♂ ただの遊びだったんだ?
Stop playing these games.	**Gomakasu-no-wa yamete-yo.** ♀ ごまかすのは止めてよ。
	Gomakasu-no-wa yamero-yo. ♂ ごまかすのは止めろよ。

This means something like "Stop trying to hide the truth," "Don't change the subject," and "Stop acting like nothing happened" all rolled into one.

Stop nagging. (better for girls)	**Gocha-gocha iwanaide-yo.** ごちゃごちゃ言わないでよ。

Gata-gata iwanaide-yo. ♀
がたがた言わないでよ。

Gocha-gocha iuna. ♂
ごちゃごちゃ言うな。

Gata-gata iuna. ♂
がたがた言うな。

We did it only once.　Ikkai yatta dake-desho. ♀
一回やっただけでしょ。

Ikkai yatta dake-darō. ♂
一回やっただけだろう。

Don't act like my husband!　Teishu-zura shinaide! ♀
亭主づらしないで！

Don't act like my wife!　Nyōbō-zura suruna! ♂
女房づらするな！

Don't act like I'm yours.　Wagamono-gao shinaide. ♀
我が物顔しないで。

Wagamono-gao suruna. ♂
我が物顔するな。

I've had it!　Mō takusan!
もうたくさん！

For extra emphasis stop abruptly on the "n."

I need more excitement and passion.　Motto shigeki ga hoshii-no/hoshiin-da. ♀/♂
もっと刺激が欲しいの／欲しいんだ。

You don't excite me anymore.　Mō doki-doki shinai.
もうドキドキしない。

Anata-ni-wa mō doki-doki shinai-no. ♀
あなたにはもうドキドキしないの。

Mō sosorarenai.
もうそそられない。

Kimi-ni-wa mō doki-doki shinai. ♂
君にはもうドキドキしない。

I don't feel sexually attracted to you anymore.

Mō sōiu kibun-ni nara-nai.
もうそういう気分にならない。

This literally means "I don't feel that way anymore," or more directly, "I don't feel like having sex with you anymore."

You're so awkward in bed.

Bukiyō.
不器用。

I wish you had more experience.

Motto keiken hōfu nara ii-noni.
もっと経験豊富なら良いのに。

You aren't any good in bed.

Sekkusu-ga heta-nano-yo/ nanda-yo. ♀/♂
セックスが下手なのよ／なんだよ。

You mean nothing (to me).

Anata-no sonzai-wa muimi. ♀
あなたの存在は無意味。

Kimi-no sonzai-wa muimi. ♂
君の存在は無意味。

I'm glad we broke up.　Wakarete yokkatta.
別れてよかった。

(Pack your stuff and) hit the road!　Mō dete-itte!
もう出て行って！

Give me back the apartment/car key.　Apāto/kuruma-no kagi-o kaeshite-yo. ♀
アパート／車のかぎを返してよ。

Apāto/kuruma-no kagi-o kaese-yo. ♂
アパート／車のかぎを返せよ。

Give me back all the presents I gave to you.　Atashi-ga ageta-mono zembu kaeshite-yo. ♀
あたしがあげた物全部返してよ。

Boku-ga ageta-mono zembu kaese-yo. ♂
僕があげた物全部返せよ。

I've already thrown them away.　Mō suteta(wa)-yo. ♀
もう捨てた（わ）よ。

Mō suteta-yo.
もう捨てたよ。

Why did you do such a thing?　Nan-de son'na-koto shita-no? ♀
何でそんな事したの？

Nan-de son'na-koto shitanda-yo? ♂
何でそんな事したんだよ？

(Because) I wanted to forget you.

Anata-o wasureta-katta
(kara). ♀
あなたを忘れたかった（から）。

Kimi-o wasureta-katta
(kara). ♂
君を忘れたかった（から）。

Don't do such a thing.

Son'na-koto shinaide.
そんな事しないで。

(You're such a) worrier.

Shimpai-shō.
心配性。

(You're such a) crybaby.

Naki-mushi.
泣きむし。

You're such a pussy.
(to a guy)

Yowa-mushi
弱虫。

You're such a bitch.

Saitei-na on'na-dana.
最低な女だな。

I didn't think you would be like this.

Kon'na hito-to-wa
omowana-katta.
こんな人とは思わなかった。

I thought you would be more mature about it.

Motto otona-no taiō
shite-kureru-to omotteta.
もっと大人の対応してくれる
と思ってた。

Grow up.

Kodomo dayo-ne.
子供だよね。

You need to be realistic.

Motto genjitsu-teki-ni kangaete-mite.
もっと現実的に考えてみて。

This is for the best.

Kore-ga tadashii sentaku nandayo.
これが正しい選択なんだよ。

I'm not your plaything.

Atashi-wa omocha-janai. ♀
あたしはおもちゃじゃない。

Boku-wa omocha-janai. ♂
僕はおもちゃじゃない。

Don't think that I'm only yours.

Atashi-wa anata-dake-no mono-janai-wayo. ♀
あたしはあなただけの物じゃないわよ。

Boku-wa kimi-dake-no mono-janai-yo. ♂
僕は君だけの物じゃないよ。

I don't belong to you.

Atashi-wa anata-no kanojo-janai. ♀
あたしはあなたの彼女じゃない。

Boku-wa kimi-no kareshi-janai. ♂
僕は君の彼氏じゃない。

Now I'll feel better (because we broke up).

Kore-de sukkiri-shita.
これですっきりした。

Literally means "I'm refreshed because of what happened."

You said bad things about me.	Atashi-no waruguchi itta-deshō? ♀ あたしの悪口言ったでしょう？ Boku-no waruguchi itta-darō? ♂ 僕の悪口言っただろう？
How can you talk (to me) like that?	Nande son'na-fū-ni ieru-no? ♀ 何でそんなふうに言えるの？ Nande son'na-fū-ni ierunda-yo? ♂ 何でそんなふうに言えるんだよ？
You talk down to me.	Itsumo watashi/boku-o mikudasu-yo-ne. いつも私／僕を見下すよね。
You talk to me like I'm a fool.	Itsumo watashi/boku-o baka-ni suru-yo-ne. いつも私／僕をバカにするよね。
Who cares?	Dare-ga son'na-koto ki-ni suru-noyo? ♀ 誰がそんな事気にするのよ？ Dare-ga son'na-koto ki-ni surunda-yo? ♂ 誰がそんな事気にするんだよ？

I hate you!	**Anata/Anta-nante kirai!** ♀ あなた／あんたなんて嫌い！ **Omae-nante kirai-dayo!** ♂ お前なんて嫌いだよ！
I can find someone better than you.	**Anata-yori ii hito-nante takusan iru-wa.** ♀ あなたよりいい人なんてたくさんいるわ。 **Kimi-yori ii ko-nante takusan iru-yo.** ♂ 君よりいい子なんてたくさんいるよ。
Who would want you?	**Dare-ga anata/anta-to tsukiau-noyo?** ♀ 誰があなた／あんたと付き合うのよ？ **Dare-ga kimi/omae-to tsukiaunda-yo?** ♂ 誰が君／お前と付き合うんだよ？
You're not the only boy in this world.	**Anata/Anta-no hoka-ni-mo otoko-nante takusan iru-wayo.** ♀ あなた／あんたの他にも男なんてたくさんいるわよ。
You're not the only girl in this would.	**Kimi/Omae-no hoka-ni-mo on'na nante takusan irunda-yo.** ♂ 君／お前の他にも女なんてたくさんいるんだよ。

You can't find anyone better than me.	Atashi-yori ii on'na-ga iru-to omotteru-no? ♀ あたしよりいい女 がいると思ってるの？ Boku-yori ii otoko-ga iru-to omotteru-no-ka? ♂ 僕よりいい男がいると思ってるのか？
I can see whomever I want/do whatever I want.	Atashi-wa yaritai yō-ni suru-wa. ♀ あたしはやりたいようにするわ。 Boku-wa yaritai yō-ni suru-yo. ♂ 僕はやりたいようにするよ。
Do it!	Sure-ba! すれば！ Shiro-yo! ♂ しろよ！
Go find yourself a new boyfriend/girlfriend.	Atarashii kanojo sagaseba. ♀ 新しい彼女探せば。 Atarashii kareshi sagase-yo. ♂ 新しい彼氏探せよ。
I've been lying to you/cheated on you.	Uso tsuiteta. 嘘ついてた。 Damashiteta. だましてた。

I haven't been completely honest with you.	Uso tsuiteta. 嘘ついてた。
I am not cut out to be in a serious relationship.	Majime-na renai-wa muri-nano/nanda. ♀/♂ 真面目な恋愛は無理なの／なんだ。
I really did try to change.	Kawaru doryoku-wa shitanda-yo. 変わる努力はしたんだよ。
I don't want to believe that.	Shinji-taku-nai. 信じたくない。
Cheater/Two-timer!	Uwaki-mono! 浮気者！

Uwaki-mono literally means "floating mind," and is usually combined with other insults, such as...

You're the worst!	Saitei! 最低！
	Saiaku! 最悪！
I have another boyfriend/girlfriend.	Hoka-ni kareshi-ga iru-no. ♀ 他に彼氏がいるの。
	Hoka-ni kanojo-ga irun-da. ♂ 他に彼女がいるんだ。

I've tried to tell you many times, but I couldn't.	Nankai-mo iō-to shitanda-kedo. 何回も言おうとしたんだけど。
I know you're seeing someone else.	Futamata kaketerun-deshō/darō? ♀ 二股かけてるんでしょう／だろう？
I've seen you checking other girls/guys out.	Hoka-no-ko/otoko-no-koto sōiu-me-de miteta-no shitteru. 他の子／男のことそういう目で見てたの知ってる。
I saw you with another girl/guy last Sunday	Senshū-no nichi-yōbi hoka-no-on'na/otoko-to issho-ni ita-no mitan-dakara/dayo. ♀/♂ 先週の日曜日他の女／男と一緒にいたの見たんだから／だよ。
Who was she/he?	Ano on'na/otoko dare? ♀/♂ あの女／男誰？
She/He was no one.	Dare-demo nai-yo. 誰でもないよ。
She/He is just a. friend/coworker	Tadano tomodachi dōryō dayo. ただの友達／同僚だよ。
You have to believe me.	Shinjite-yo. 信じてよ。

I don't believe you.

Shinji-rarenai.
信じられない。

Shinjite-kure-yo. ♂
信じてくれよ。

I believed in you, yet you tricked me.

Shinjiteta-noni damashita deshō. ♀
信じてたのにだましたでしょう。

Shinjiteta-noni damashita darō. ♂
信じてたのにだましただろう。

Choose: her/him or me.

Dotchi-ga suki-nano?
どっちが好きなの？

Dotchi-ni suru-no?
どっちにするの

I won't forgive you.

Anata-o yurusanai. ♀
あなたを許さない。

Kimi-o yurusanai. ♂
君を許さない。

Be nice to your new sweetheart.

Atarashii kanojo-to nakayoku-ne. ♀
新しい彼女と仲良くね。

Atarashii kareshi-to nakayoku-na. ♂
新しい彼氏と仲良くな。

I hope she/he can make you happy.

Shiawase-ni-ne.
幸せにね。

Don't make her/him sad.	Kanojo/Kareshi-o nakase-cha dame-dayo. 彼女／彼氏を泣かせちゃだめだよ。
Have you already decided (which one)?	Mō kimeta? もう決めた？
Don't make promises you can't keep.	Mamore-nai yakusoku-wa shinaide. 守れない約束はしないで。
I can't stand it.	Mō tae-rarenai. もうたえられない。
You never came over.	Kona-katta deshō. ♀ 来なかったでしょう。 Kona-katta darō. ♂ 来なかっただろう。
You left me (stranded) (at...).	(...-ni) oitetta deshō. ♀ (…に)おいてったでしょう。 (...-ni) oitetta darō. ♂ (…に)おいてっただろう。
You left without telling me.	Nani-mo iwanai-de itchatta. 何も言わないで行っちゃった。
I can't forget my ex.	Moto-kano/kare-o wasure-rarenai. 元カノ／彼を忘れられない。

Kano カノ is short for **kanojo** (girlfriend), and **kare** 彼 is short for **kareshi** (boyfriend).

I can't forget her/him.   (Moto-kanojo/kareshi-o)
wasure-rarenai.
(元彼女／彼氏を)忘れられない。

I can't forgive her/him.   (Moto-kanojo/kareshi-o)
yuruse-nai.
(元彼女／彼氏を)許せない。

I know it's fruitless.   Muda-nano-wa wakatteru.
無駄なのは分かってる。

I am a fool.   Hontō-ni baka-dayo-ne.
本当にバカだよね。

I'm so sorry.   Hontō-ni gomen.
本当にごめん。

I was so happy with you.   Hontō-ni shiawase datta.
本当に幸せだった。

I really did love you.   Hontō-ni suki datta.
本当に好きだった。

I will never forget you.   Isshō wasurenai-kara.
一生忘れないから。

I wish you happiness.   Shiawase-ni natte-ne.
幸せになってね。